BATTLE FOR THE
NORTH ATLANTIC

THE STRATEGIC NAVAL CAMPAIGN
THAT WON WORLD WAR II IN EUROPE

JOHN R. BRUNING

CRESTLINE

Quarto is the authority on a wide range of topics.

Quarto educates, entertains and enriches the lives of our readers—enthusiasts and lovers of hands-on living.

www.quartoknows.com

This edition published in 2017 by
Crestline
an imprint of Book Sales
a division of Quarto Publishing Group USA Inc.
142 West 36th Street 4th Floor
New York, New York 10018
USA

All images are official U.S. archives photos from the author's collection unless otherwise noted.

Maps by Phillip Schwartzberg, Meridian Mapping

ISBN-13: 978-0-7858-3512-7

Editor: Scott Pearson
Design Manager: James Kegley
Design: Simon Larkin
Layout: Chris Fayers

10 9 8 7 6 5 4 3 2 1

On the front cover: Photo illustration of an Atlantic convoy. *U.S. Coast Guard and Shutterstock*

On the back cover: A U.S. tanker and a German U-boat sinking into the Atlantic.

On the frontis: An American battleship pitches through heavy seas during World War II. The Atlantic was among the most dangerous and inhospitable places on the planet.

On the table of contents: Atlantic convoy ships being shielded by the U.S. Coast Guard cutter Spencer. *U.S. Coast Guard*

Printed in China

FSC
www.fsc.org
MIX
Paper from
responsible sources
FSC® C101537

For Col. Robert Ault, whose empathy and intellect is an inspiration.

For Sgt. Scott Tant, whose talents with a Nikon I sought to emulate, but could never match.

For Capt. Cassie Wyllie, whose fire conquers every challenge.

For Andrew Alvord, the fighting quartermaster who taught me flexibility
is a key to victory in whatever we do.

And for Ed and Renee, who keep me moving forward.
You are the reason I can write again.

CONTENTS

Acknowledgments

In almost twenty years of writing, I've never encountered a project more difficult than *The Battle for the North Atlantic*. The campaign in the Atlantic is so vast and rich, full of fascinating stories and epic battles, that trying to figure out what to include, what to exclude, and when to stop researching became the first of a series of major challenges.

In 2010, as I was researching this book, I had the chance to deploy to Afghanistan and embed with U.S. forces there. I snapped up the opportunity, thinking that between missions I could work on the Atlantic campaign. It would be a great diversion from modern combat. I was absolutely out of my mind thinking that.

Twelve- to twenty-hour days left me exhausted to the bone. In September 2010, I flew about a hundred hours operationally with the helicopter crews of Task Force Brawler. I went out on ground patrols and flew to Helmand Province to embed with the 162 Engineers (Oregon National Guard) as they carried out their deployment's final route clearance operation for the USMC units in the area.

Somehow I did find time to sit down and start this book in my dusty hooch at FOB Shank. That's when the Taliban intervened. It became almost comical. Every time I started typing, the enemies of the free world would lob a rocket onto our base, sending us to the bunkers as the incoming claxon rang out—always after the fact. After sitting in the dark with Afghan National Army (ANA) guys flagging us with their rifles, I gave up on the bunkers and stayed in my hooch. Between this book and steak night, we were virtually guaranteed to be hit by the enemy.

When I came home from Afghanistan, every possible home fire was burning. I spent the next seven months taking care of my wife, Jennifer, as she went through treatment for thyroid cancer. At times, I worked on this book at Oregon Health Sciences University as she slept following surgery. When I could, I would escape to the Cascades and write in a friend's cabin far away from cell phones and internet connections. I crawled along with this book, knocking down a chapter here, a chapter there as I worked through creating my new sense of normalcy following Afghanistan. It took two years to finish, the longest project of my writing career since I spent five years turning my master's thesis into *Jungle Ace* back in the 1990s.

The Battle for the North Atlantic was written all over the world: Afghanistan; Kuwait; Germany; Capitola, California; the Cascade Mountains; Fort Hoskins in the Coast Range; and even in an old Cold War USAF air defense intercept station, complete with a fallout shelter still stocked with civil defense rations from the early sixties.

There is no way this book could have been finished without the extreme patience and understanding of Erik Gilg and Scott Pearson. Long-suffering, they rode my many waves waiting for the manuscript and could have canceled the book more than once. To them, I owe a huge debt. Thank you, guys. I appreciate the slack you cut me.

Richard Kane brought this project to me initially, and it was his belief that I was the writer to put it to page that set me to work on it. Richard's been a vital part of my career over the years. I think we've worked on six books together. Thank you, my friend, for all you've done for me.

To my kids, Ed and Renee: you both have sacrificed so much for me. I cannot tell you how proud of you I am and how vital your support has been. I'm frankly tired of missing events and saying I have to work instead of playing with the two of you. The years ahead will be different, I promise.

My life has changed radically since 2010 when I first took this book on. My new sense of normalcy required letting go of so much of value to my old life. Yet, ultimately I gained far more than I have lost. That is due in large part to the unique bond I share with Allison Serventi Morgan. Allison holds a master's in military history and is an expert on military technology, code-breaking, and the Ultra secret. I turned to her for help on this aspect of the U-boat war, and she wrote much of those sections of the book with me, including the Bletchley Park sidebars. Collaborating with a person I admire and respect was an incredible experience. I look forward to many, many more opportunities to work together in the years ahead.

People come and go in your life, but those few who stick through the decades are the reason why life has meaning. Allison, you're that person for me. From that first chance meeting at Redwood in 1981, through grad night, reconnecting years later, and all we've shared these past three years, you've been the sustaining presence in my life. Thank you for all you've done for me.

I dedicated this book to some truly exceptional Americans. Cassie Wyllie, Rob Ault, Andrew Alvord, and Scott Tant are all U.S. soldiers I met when I embedded with Task Force Brawler at FOB Shank. Through them, I witnessed their compassion, devotion, and courage in extreme situations. They showed me firsthand what it takes to fight for our country, something I'd written about a great deal, but never understood until I witnessed them in action. They are the best of us: intelligent, driven, engaging. They learned how to balance bravery and violence of action with leaps of faith and mercy. They steered a difficult path through insurgency and incoming; in doing so they found unlikely allies willing to join our cause. Scott Tant documented it all as one

of the best combat photographers serving in the U.S. Army today. Andrew Alvord stepped out of his role as quartermaster to lead men in battle as the commander of Colonel Ault's ground combat platoon. In August 2010, he and his men helped save an engineer convoy that had come under attack.

Colonel Ault is a blend of extraordinary intellect and natural leader. Where he goes, people eagerly follow. I trusted him with my life and never doubted once that when and if the chips were down, he'd always make the right call. He is the consummate professional, a man who understands that insurgencies are not won by killing, but by forging relationships by accepting others on their own terms. He is the type of officer we need leading our nation at its highest levels someday.

Cassie Wyllie is a new breed of warrior this country needs to know more about. One of two female Apache pilots in the 3rd Combat Aviation Brigade, Cassie has internal fires that burn white hot. Resolute, determined, she blasted through every obstacle, every bit of adversity she encountered to blaze a trail for others to follow. I saw her in action over a remote outpost in the Hindu Kush, and I will forever be grateful to her for laying down the fire we needed to get in and out of that miserable place. Cassie, you're a game changer in all you do.

Andrew, Scott, Rob, and Cassie—there are times I despaired and wondered if I'd ever be able to write again after we lost Spc. Taylor Marks. I came to Afghanistan lost and looking for purpose. Meeting you helped me recommit and return home to write again. This book would have remained a wishful dream had that not happened. Thank you for showing me the path again.

Introduction

They fought and died in desperate battles played out in the most unforgiving place on the planet. Some wore their nation's uniform, but most were civilians who went to sea in hopes of escaping the Great Depression. Instead, they found themselves in the middle of a titanic struggle upon which hinged the course of history. By the time the shooting stopped, 3,500 of their ships lay beneath the Atlantic Ocean's gray-green swells.

These men fought with outdated equipment in poorly armed ships whose ancient engines wheezed them along at pathetic speeds. When alone, they were easy prey for the Axis vessels hunting them. When their ships succumbed to a submarine-fired torpedo, or a marauding surface raider, they died in horrifying ways. Those who survived to reach the water faced another ordeal. Clinging to bits of wreckage or huddled against the elements in lifeboats, they endured a slow death on the churning seas. Too many watched as friendly ships vanished on the horizon, their captains too fearful of the U-boat menace to risk their rescue. They died of hypothermia, starvation, and dehydration, lost among the bitter seas.

This is their story, told by the men who had the courage to ride with them and photograph their crucible. Many of these photographers died in action. Those who survived gave successive generations a tremendous gift. Their willingness to risk everything produced a record of images that, when pieced together, form a vivid mosaic of the war's longest campaign.

This was a campaign overshadowed by such events as Monty's stand at Alamein, or Patton's race across France.

It lingered in the background as Paris fell, England stood alone, and Russia bled. It was all but forgotten by the time of D-Day and the crossing of the Rhine. Yet control of the Atlantic was the foundation for everything that unfolded after 1939. The convoys became the machinery that held the Allied cause together. The Axis came close several times to destroying it, but could never deliver a decisive blow.

It was a war of statistics, of tonnage lost, ships constructed, and cargo delivered. In some ways, it was far more mathematically driven than any other aspect of World War II. In that tapestry of indicators, the human element has tended to get lost. Few remember the eighty thousand sailors for whom the cold Atlantic became their grave.

The Allied merchant mariners saved nations, yet history has shafted them. Despite all the ink devoted to World War II, students of the era would be hard pressed to name even one of these civilian warriors. The men who guided the merchant ships across the Atlantic remain the war's faceless martyrs. Without their tenacity, a dark age would have engulfed the Western world, and millions more would have perished. Their blood bought a future for all of us. But when the last shell splash settled, their efforts were ignored by thankless Western governments.

This is their story, told with the images taken by equally anonymous photographers who ranged across this hellish aquatic battlefield side by side with the men who carried home the Allied victory.

Top left: Civilians of all ages played the key role in the Atlantic campaign. Without the men of the merchant marine, the weapons, supplies, and raw materials needed to defeat the Axis would never have been brought to bear. Here, May Jones, a sixty-eight-year-old British merchant sailor, mans a machine gun aboard his cargo vessel prior to making the Atlantic crossing. *Top right:* Merchant seamen from across the globe, of every race, creed, and color, participated in the Battle of the Atlantic. There was no distinction made in the bitter fighting that raged for six years on the cold, gray swells between America and England. *Bottom left:* German sailors serving aboard the Reich's submarines and surface fleet fought with dogged determination until their nation's final defeat. *Bottom right:* Sailors clean an antiaircraft gun aboard a troop transport prior to departure for the Atlantic crossing. Long-range German bombers, such as the Focke-Wulf Fw-200 Kondor, took a heavy toll of Allied shipping until air cover could be provided for the convoys. Antiaircraft weapons could also be used against U-boats as they launched night surface attacks against Allied ships.

Above: A deck load of American troops aboard an Allied transport wearing lifebelts. For thousands of men whose ships were torpedoed, those lifebelts proved of little use in the frigid Atlantic waters where hypothermia could kill in mere minutes. *Below:* The primary German weapon in the Atlantic war: a Type VII U-boat. These mass-produced vessels were cramped and miserable for their crews, but they were formidable opponents for the Allies. *Opposite:* A freighter loaded with ammunition takes a torpedo hit during a U-boat attack. Few men survived such sudden, violent attacks as their ships became instant infernos.

CHAPTER ONE

THE FIRST INNING

3 SEPTEMBER, 1939, AFTERNOON

The young staff officer burst into the conference room, interrupting a daily status meeting. Admiral Karl Doenitz, Germany's aggressive and capable commander of its U-boat force, looked up to see the staffer holding a teletype message. He handed it to Doenitz. It was a message from German naval signals intelligence, otherwise known as B-Dienst. Listening stations had picked up a Royal Navy radio transmission that said, "Most immediate to all his majesty's ships: TOTAL GERMANY repetition TOTAL GERMANY." B-Dienst decrypted the signal and got it to Doenitz as quickly as possible.

The German admiral crumpled the teletype message and muttered, "My God! So it's war with England again!"

He left the conference room without another word. He knew the score. In 1918, he'd commanded a U-boat. He had fought the Royal Navy and had lost. Blown to the surface during a fight, he and his crew were forced to surrender.

The Royal Navy would be his enemy a second time, though Hitler had assured him that there would be no war with Britain until the mid-1940s. Germany's navy needed time to rebuild and rearm after the Versailles Treaty banned the Reich from having a blue water force. Plan Z, which had been undertaken only a short time before this crisis moment, would have built the new Kriegsmarine into a powerful force of 13 ultra-modern battleships, 4 carriers, 33 swift cruisers, and more than 250 submarines.

Plan Z had been overcome by events. Twenty-one submarines, a few pocket battleships designed for raider operations, a couple of cruisers, and some destroyers—that was all the German navy could wield against the nation that ruled the gray Atlantic. For a realist like Doenitz, he knew his men faced long odds. He also recognized that the pace of new construction was so slow that it would be years before he could field enough submarines to starve Britain out of the war.

For thirty minutes, he sought solitude in his austere headquarters outside of Wilhelmshaven. Finally composed, he returned to the conference room, where he set the tone for the trial ahead. To his staff, he announced, "This war will last a long time, but if each does his duty we will win."

Opposite: U-boat Flotilla One during a commissioning ceremony in 1935. The Treaty of Versailles that ended World War I had prohibited the Germans from having a submarine force, but after Hitler rose to power in 1933, such limitations were ignored.

Facing the Kriegsmarine's two battleships, three pocket battleships, five cruisers, and seventeen destroyers was a British fleet that consisted of six aircraft carriers, fifteen battlewagons, sixty-eight cruisers, and hundreds of destroyers. That didn't include the French, who could contribute several more capital ships and escorts with their Atlantic fleet.

The numbers were deceptive. The British fleet of 1939 was a shadow of its former glory. The post–World War I years saw Great Britain racked with debt, economic stagnation, and slashed budgets. The Royal Navy withered, its ships growing older with no replacements in sight. The naval arms limitation treaties artificially preserved Britain's superiority on the seas, but at the cost of the industries required to sustain a modern fleet. By the late 1930s, most of the manufacturers who specialized in naval armaments, turrets, and other key components had succumbed to the Great Depression's stringent budgets. When the British sought to rearm in

the mid-1930s, they did not have the industrial base needed to quickly build a modernized fleet.

Most of the Royal Navy's battle line consisted of ancient, R-class warships that could barely make twenty-one knots. Only a few had been modernized by 1939, and in the intervening years between the wars, only the battleships *Rodney* and *Nelson* had been launched. These two vessels turned out to be riddled with design flaws that limited their operational performance.

The Fleet Air Arm was in worse shape. The Royal Air Force controlled naval aviation in the interwar years; its obsession with strategic bombing meant the FAA received the worst manufacturers and the least funds. When the war began, the Fleet Air Arm was largely equipped with abysmal aircraft designs.

The antisubmarine forces had also been neglected. The Admiralty believed that the development of sonar (called ASDIC by the British) would handily deal with the undersea menace. As a result, what scarce funds

German troops construct a bridge across a river during the invasion of Poland.

Grand Admiral Raeder, commander of the German navy, during an inspection visit. Hitler gradually lost all faith in Raeder as the Reich's surface ships failed to perform as hoped.

were available went to construct more glamorous ships. Few admirals wanted to divert funds for thousand-ton convoy escorts that could barely plod along at seventeen or eighteen knots. It just wasn't a priority.

On September 3, 1939, the Royal Navy was desperately short of antisubmarine vessels. New construction programs would be undertaken, but the British yards were already overcommitted. Basic war materials were also in short supply. The British steel industry could not produce enough armor plating to support the new naval construction program, which included five new battleships and four new aircraft carriers. In the mid-1930s, the British had to order fifteen thousand tons of armor plating from the Czechs.

Antiaircraft guns were another significant Royal Navy shortcoming as homegrown designs had met with total failure. The British turned to the Swedes and purchased 40mm Bofors guns to fill the need for a medium AA gun. The Swiss provided the 20mm Oerlikon design for close-in defense. Yet even as these new weapons reached the fleet, their effectiveness was compromised by the slow and inaccurate antiaircraft fire control system the Royal Navy installed on its vessels. Worse, the systems themselves were produced in such small quantities that some of the warships reaching the fleet had yet to receive them.

There were other shortcomings. The Royal Navy armed its latest destroyers with dual-purpose 4.7-inch guns. This gave the British tin cans significant versatility, which was compromised by a technical flaw. The guns could only be elevated thirty degrees, which was not high enough to hit incoming dive bombers.

It would take time and combat experience for these errors to be corrected. In the meantime, both sides

went to war with the fleets they had in 1939. From the outset, the clash in the Atlantic was a brutal one.

Just in case the invasion of Poland triggered a larger war, Doenitz had sent his few U-boats to sea at the end of August. With war, Hitler now ordered him to observe the international rules of prize warfare. Prize warfare forced the U-boats to throw away their greatest assets— surprise and stealth. Instead of torpedoing a passing ship while submerged, or at least while the target was unaware, the U-boat commanders had to make their attacks on the surface and secure the safety of the merchant ship's crew. Ships flying neutral flags were out of bounds and could not be attacked. Hitler's intent behind the order was to avoid antagonizing neutrals like the United States.

But Oberleutnant Fritz-Julius Lemp, *U-30*'s twenty-six-year-old skipper, had a reputation for informality and snap judgments. He chafed against rules and tended to be emotional. In some ways, he had the temperament of an artist—charismatic and well-regarded by his crew, but moody and prone to outbursts of anger.

Above: Admiral Karl Doenitz was an old submariner and veteran of the first Atlantic campaign during World War I. He was captured while commanding *UB-68* after British escorts drove his boat to the surface in 1918. In World War II, he became the driving force behind Germany's U-boat campaign in the Atlantic. *Below:* HMS *Barham*, a *Queen Elizabeth*–class battleship, was one of the mainstays of the Royal Navy's interwar fleet.

Coastal submarines of U-boat Flotilla Neustadt, seen prior to the war's outbreak. These Type IIB boats were designed as training platforms as the German navy rebuilt its undersea fleet. When the war broke out, many of the Type II's were pressed into service. *U-7*, the boat second from the right, sank three ships during six combat patrols during the war. The boat and its twenty-six crewmen were lost during a diving accident in 1944.

On the war's first evening, Lemp's *U-30* encountered the Donaldson Atlantic Line's *Athenia* as it steamed for Montreal, Canada. *Athenia* had departed Glascow the day the Germans invaded Poland, making stops at Belfast and Liverpool before setting sail across the Atlantic with 1,103 passengers aboard, including 300 Jewish refugees and some Americans.

While surfaced, Lemp spotted the liner about 250 miles northwest of Ireland. *U-30* submerged to periscope depth and Lemp fired a spread of torpedoes. Aboard *Athenia*, the passengers had just sat down to dinner when a violent explosion rocked their ship. One of Lemp's torpedoes had struck next to the engine room.

Athenia went dead in the water and began to sink. Lemp ordered *U-30* to the surface and sent his deck gun crews forward to try to destroy *Athenia*'s radio mast with shellfire before she could report his position. While on the surface, he saw women and children running in panic on the decks and recognized his mistake. His surprise attack had violated the führer's orders.

He ordered his boat down, even as his crew could hear the terrified screams of women and children. Lemp went deep and did not radio a contact report. Meanwhile, 118 people died, including 22 Americans.

This was the sort of action that had outraged President Woodrow Wilson and drove America into the Great War. British propaganda seized on the incident. The United States registered its outrage. The Germans launched an information counterattack, masterminded by Joseph Goebbels, who claimed that the British sank

Above: A Saro Lerwick long-range maritime reconnaissance bomber of 209 Squadron takes off from Loch Ryan, Scotland. The Lerwick was supposed to join Coastal Command as a stable mate of the Short Sunderland, but its high accident rate, poor performance, and inability to fly on one engine condemned the design. It saw very limited service and was replaced by Lend-Lease Consolidated PBY Catalinas by mid-1941. Lerwicks attacked two U-boats during the war, both of which escaped unharmed. *Below:* A Dornier Do-24 maritime patrol aircraft. The Luftwaffe was woefully short of such aircraft throughout the war, and political infighting between Herman Goering, Admiral Raeder, and Doenitz hindered cooperation between the German air force and navy.

Left: Fritz-Julius Lemp (left wearing the Knight's Cross) meets with Admiral Doenitz. As the unorthodox commander of *U-30*, he sank almost a hundred thousand tons of Allied shipping. *Below: Ark Royal* (in background), one of the most modern Royal Navy fleet carriers at the start of the war.

their own ship to make the Third Reich look bad and inflame U.S. sentiment.

Lemp returned to Germany a few weeks later and delivered his report. He claimed he thought the *Athenia* was a troop ship. To cover up the incident, *U-30*'s logbook was sanitized, the entries dealing with the attack deleted or rewritten. The entire crew was also sworn to secrecy.

Truth was, Lemp was ahead of his time. In the months to come, the gentleman's war Hitler had hoped to fight in the Atlantic turned ugly and cruel. By its nature, it could be no other way.

Above: A German army machine gun crew practices a river assault crossing. *Below:* A German artillery crew in action during the Polish campaign.

At the outset of the war, many U-boat skippers displayed mercy and kindness to their victims. That changed after *U-156* sank the SS Laconia off the West Africa coast in September 1942. As the ship sank, almost two thousand civilians, Allied soldiers, and Italian prisoners of war ended up in the water. *U-156* and *U-506* tried to rescue the survivors, only to be attacked by a U.S. Army Air Force B-24. After that, Doenitz forbade his crews from rescue attempts in what became known as the Laconia Order. That order served as the basis for postwar prosecution of Doenitz for war crimes. In this remarkable photograph, *U-506*'s crew rescues *Laconia*'s desperate survivors.

Two days after the *Athenia* went down, Gunther Prien's *U-47* encountered a 2,400-ton freighter in the Bay of Biscay. Owned by the Cunard Line, the vessel lacked the speed to escape from the German submarine. Observing the rules of prize warfare, Prien ran the ship down on the surface. A shot across the bow failed to halt the vessel, so *U-47*'s gunners put six shells into her.

As the crew abandoned the freighter, Prien cruised alongside the lifeboats and spotted a wounded man and ordered his crew to give him a shot of brandy. When

a Norwegian steamer appeared, Prien signaled it and asked its captain to take his target's crew aboard. After the Norwegians had fished everyone out of the water, Prien delivered the coup de grace on the freighter with a couple of well-placed torpedoes.

Despite the constrictive rules of engagement, Germany's submariners scored some stunning successes. That September, the Royal Navy employed its fleet carriers for antisubmarine work, which was like using battleships to hunt PT boats. The risk was

A *Nelson*-class battleship, the first of the post–World War I designs completed by the British. Dubbed "Treaty Battleships," *Nelson* and *Rodney* were unorthodox ships, as their nine 16-inch guns and secondary batteries were located aft. Both ships of this class were found to be hard to maneuver and tough to dock, and their main guns had a restrictive field of fire. Nevertheless, both battleships served the duration of the war, taking part in some of the most important surface engagements of the Atlantic campaign.

simply not worth the reward, and such an employment of capital ships could only end in disaster.

On September 17, 1939, Leutnant Otto Schuhart's *U-29* caught HMS *Courageous* in the Western Approaches. The twenty-six thousand–ton flat-top was protected only by a pair of destroyers, so it was not hard for *U-29* to penetrate the screen and close to three thousand yards. Two of Schuhart's torpedoes struck the flat-top, which sank with more than five hundred of her sailors.

A month later, on the night of October 17, 1939, Gunther Prien guided *U-47* into the British fleet anchorage at Scapa Flow. Prien had reconnoitered the approaches while on a prewar vacation. Aerial photographs of the Scapa Flow antisubmarine measures assisted the crew as *U-47* crept past a sunken block ship in a channel the British thought was secure.

The Home Fleet rode at anchor that night as Prien's boat crept up on the battleship *Royal Oak*. His initial attack scored a torpedo hit on the battlewagon's bow. The British thought there'd been some sort of internal explosion. That mistake allowed Prien to back away, reload his forward torpedo tubes, and return to fire another spread. This time, the *Royal Oak* suffered catastrophic damage and sank at her mooring in fifteen minutes. About 330 men died.

Prien escaped the Scapa Flow to return home as the Kriegsmarine's first war hero, becoming known as the "bull of Scapa Flow" after the snorting bull painted on his U-boat's conning tower by the victorious crew. At a later press conference, the Germans introduced their submarine ace to the world. American journalist William Shirer, who was present that day, observed that Prien was "capable . . . clean-cut, cocky . . . a fanatical Nazi."

By the end of October, Doenitz's men had sunk twenty-seven ships and destroyed eleven more with mines. Including the Luftwaffe's air-sea attacks, the first two months of the war saw the British lose sixty-eight merchant ships. In return, the British sank seven U-boats, killing about 350 men. Losing a third of his command in two months alarmed Doenitz. He knew if it continued, his force would be broken before it could affect the outcome of the war.

After the surviving boats returned to Germany to rearm and refuel, the Kriegsmarine couldn't sustain the

Above: Gunter Prien's *U-47* returns to Germany after sinking *Royal Oak* in Scapa Flow. Here, the crew of the cruiser *Emden* welcomes Prien's home.
Below: After Scapa Flow, Prien became the face of the U-boat force in Germany. Hailed as a hero, he was treated to parades and feted by Nazi officials. He would go on to become one of the most successful submarine commanders of World War II.

HMS *Furious*, the Royal Navy's first aircraft carrier. Based on a battle cruiser hull, *Furious* joined the fleet at the end of World War I. After receiving a full flight deck in the 1920s, the flat-top saw extensive duty in the Atlantic, off Norway in 1940 and in the Arctic. She survived the war to be scrapped in 1948.

full court press it gave the British at the outset of the war. Doenitz established a rotation that would keep at least a few boats out in the Atlantic. Others would refit and rearm. The Germans settled into a battle rhythm that would serve them well in the long run, but for the near term it led to a drop in ship kills out in the Atlantic. Instead of twenty-one boats out on a patrol at any given moment, the Germans were lucky to have five. Over the next two months, the boats managed to sink forty-six ships, totaling about 130,000 tons.

As Doenitz's undersea strategy took shape, another battle raged far to the south. It was one that reflected a naval strategy almost four hundred years old.

Above: During the interwar period, the Fleet Air Arm fell under the Royal Air Force. The RAF's leadership, obsessed with strategic bombing, cared little for shipboard aviation and relegated the weakest aircraft manufacturers to the Fleet Air Arm. As a result, the FAA air crews were forced to fly inferior aircraft, such as the Blackburn Roc and Skua. The exception was the Fairey Swordfish, an obsolete design that adapted well to the rugged weather conditions of the North Atlantic. The Swordfish served as a torpedo bomber, a float-equipped reconnaissance/scout and as a night bomber. Its crews affectionately called it "The Stringbag." *Left:* Kapitänleutnant Heinrich Lehmann addresses the crew of *U-96*. Lehmann commanded *U-8* and *U-5* at the outset of the war. Later he skippered *U-96* and *U-256*, sinking twenty-four ships. He died in Bremen in 1986.

CHAPTER TWO

PHANTOMS

Throughout the 1930s, the German navy rehearsed for war against France. The nascent Kriegsmarine could never stand against such a foe as the British—every German officer knew that. Only in 1944 when Plan Z was completed could the Germans fight as equals in the North Atlantic.

Until then, the Kriegsmarine's numerical inferiority dictated the strategy Erich Raeder employed when the war began. He could not afford a Jutland-like fleet action with the British. Though his ships were more modern and more capable than the Royal Navy's, facing the Home Fleet could only lead to a German defeat.

So Raeder took an indirect approach. In conjunction with the U-boat arm, his surface fleet would conduct raiding operations against Allied sea lanes. Using fast, powerfully armed warships striking simultaneously at different points, Raeder hoped to stretch the British thin, keep them reactive, and force them to divert resources to chasing his raiders down.

At the end of August, Raeder sent the pocket battleship *Admiral Graf Spee* into the South Atlantic, where her skipper, Kapitän Hans Langsdorff (a Jutland veteran), had orders to remain hidden until activated by

Hitler. Raeder had three pocket battleships with which to pursue his commerce-raiding strategy. The *Graf Spee* deployed south. The *Deutschland* was sent to the North Atlantic, and the *Admiral Scheer* remained behind at Wilhelmshaven, where British Bristol Blenheims damaged her during an air raid on September 4, 1940. That kept *Scheer* in port until 1940.

Three weeks into the war, Hitler authorized the Kriegsmarine to commence raider operations against the Allies. On September 30, 1939, *Graf Spee* bagged her first, the SS *Clement*. Discovered off Penambuco, Brazil, the 5,050-ton tramp steamer's crew abandoned ship when the *Graf Spee*'s Arado 196 scout floatplane fired its machine gun at the vessel. After directing the crew toward the South American coast, Langsdorff's crew attempted to sink the *Clement* with explosive charges. When that failed, he ordered the ship to be sunk with torpedoes and gunfire. Much to Langsdorff's bemusement, it took two torpedo attacks, twenty-five 5.9-inch shells, and five 11-inch shells to finally sink the old scow.

The next night, *Clement*'s crew reached the Brazilian coast and reported they'd been attacked by *Admiral*

Opposite: A *Leipzig*-class light cruiser, seen here before the war. Both *Leipzig* and her improved sister ship, *Nürnberg*, survived the war despite both being torpedoed by the same British submarine in the North Sea on December 13, 1939.

Scheer. The news electrified the Royal Navy, which shuffled resources to create no fewer than eight Anglo-French hunting groups to deal with the threat. For two months, Langsdorff forced the Allies to devote four battleships, four battle cruisers, six aircraft carriers, and more than twenty cruisers to chasing him down.

What followed was a masterful game of nautical cat and mouse. Langsdorff stayed mobile, striking along the South American coast one day, then steaming east to hit the lanes from Capetown to Europe the next. He

backtracked and went silent for days at a time as he hid in the mid-Atlantic far outside normal traffic areas. Then he'd lash out again.

On October 5, the *Graf Spee* captured the 4,650-ton steamer SS *Newton Beach*, which Langsdorff used as a prison ship for the Allied merchant seamen he'd captured. That same day, the *Deutschland* discovered and sank the SS *Stonegate* four hundred miles southeast of Bermuda. At first, the British thought that the loss of both vessels was the work of only one pocket battleship.

Langsdorff struck again two days later, capturing and sinking a 4,222-ton steamer carrying sugar back to England. The German skipper decided to transfer all his prisoners to his command and sink the SS *Newton Beach*, whose slow speed was hindering his mobility.

Since the British lacked both bases and adequate numbers of patrol planes, both pocket battleships roamed the Atlantic without fear of aerial detection. The pursuit of *Graf Spee* and *Deutschland* took on all the trappings of a Napoleonic-era chase. The Allies were reduced to hunting for the two pocket battleships with the venerable Mark One eyeball. Trying to find a six hundred–foot-long steel target in an ocean that covered tens of thousands of square miles was no easy task. Not surprisingly, after capturing a second merchant ship (the SS *City of Flint*, which caused a diplomatic incident with the United States), *Deutschland* slipped through the naval cordon and returned to Germany unscathed. She'd been active in the North Atlantic for ten weeks.

Meanwhile, *Graf Spee* continued to prey on Allied vessels. During a mid-November swing into the Indian Ocean, the Langsdorff crew destroyed the SS *Africa Shell*, a small tanker.

A little over a week later, Raeder's two battle cruisers, *Scharnhorst* and *Gneisenau*, sortied into the North Atlantic on another commerce-raiding mission. They ran across part of the Royal Navy's picket line and

THE *ALTMARK* AFFAIR

The *Graf Spee* operated at sea from the end of August until December 1939, never once stopping into a port or friendly base until Kapitän Hans Langsdorff limped into Montevideo Harbor at the end of the Battle of the River Plate. When he needed provisions or fuel, Langsdorff rendezvoused with the German supply ship *Altmark*. *Altmark*, a 14,367-ton tanker, remained hidden in the middle of the South Atlantic, away from the main shipping lanes until after the *Graf Spee* was destroyed. Before his final battle, Langsdorff had transferred to the *Altmark* 303 British merchant seamen—all the men captured by his raiding exploits. Imprisoned below decks, the British sailors spent the next two months aboard the German vessel as it slowly crept north for home.

In mid-February, the *Altmark* made her dash into the North Sea and reached the Norwegian coast. The German naval personnel on board stopped wearing their uniforms, and most of the guns the British captives had seen on the voyage suddenly disappeared. The reason for this became clear later to those British aboard: the *Altmark* was trying to steal back to Germany through neutral Norwegian waters and was trying to look like an unarmed merchant ship.

The British weren't buying it. On February 14, 1940, a RAF Coastal Command reconnaissance aircraft detected the *Altmark* and reported her position. First Lord of the Admiralty Winston Churchill gave orders to intercept the vessel and board her. A Royal Navy task force composed of one cruiser and four destroyers

Left: The *Altmark*, one of *Graf Spee*'s captured prizes, was found by the Royal Navy in a Norwegian fjord in early 1940.

Above: After discovering the *Altmark*, destroyer HMS *Cossack* boarded her on the evening of February 16, 1940. The Royal Navy sailors killed six Germans of the prize crew and wounded eight others before securing the vessel.

caught up with her in Joessenfjord, not far from Stavanger. As the British ships steamed for her, two Norwegian gunboats intercepted the British and told them the *Altmark* was unarmed and had already been examined by a Norwegian boarding party the day before. The Norwegians ordered the British to leave.

The task force backed off until Churchill sent its commander, Capt. Philip Vian, a direct order to board the *Altmark* and liberate the prisoners British intelligence had learned were below decks.

That evening, HMS *Cossack* steamed swiftly into the fjord. The British brushed off a Norwegian coastal patrol vessel and pressed on to discover the *Altmark* lying in the fjord with all her deck lights blazing. Captain Vian swung parallel to the German vessel and slid alongside her. The moment their hulls scraped, a boarding party under the *Cossack*'s executive officer threw gangplanks between the two ships and poured

The British stormed aboard *Altmark* in clear violation of Norwegian neutrality. The Norwegians protested, but did little else. The Germans, enraged that some of their sailors were shot after they had jumped overboard and had tried to escape, later invoked the incident at the Nuremburg War Crime Trials after the war.

across them onto *Altmark*'s deck. The British divided into five teams, each with a specific mission. The XO led a small force to the bridge, where the first German they encountered threw his pistol away rather than fight the onrushing British sailors.

On the bridge, a hand-to-hand slugfest broke out between the German watch and the British. Both sides battled over control of *Altmark*'s engine telegraph. The Brits had discovered the engines were set to full ahead. In the middle of the fracas, they changed the telegraph to full reverse. The Germans beat back the Royal Navy sailors long enough to slam the telegraph forward once again. Unbeknownst to the *Cossack*'s crew, the Germans were trying to avoid being driven aground by the current. As the British finally subdued to the German bridge watch, that's exactly what happened. The *Altmark* went hard aground on some nearby rocks.

All over the ship, hand-to-hand fighting and point-blank firefights broke out. Several Germans jumped overboard, only to be cut down as they swam. The

British killed four German crewmembers and wounded five others before finally securing the vessel. The captured German officers admitted that there were British prisoners on board, and the *Cossack*'s crew went searching for them below decks. The XO led a team to the forward hold and discovered about half the captives there. They'd been denied food for three days and were very relieved to be rescued.

In the after hold, the rest of the British merchant seamen waited with trepidation after hearing the firefights overhead. Finally, a voice rang out, "The navy's here!" The aft hold hatch was opened, and the *Cossack*'s crew liberated the remaining prisoners. All 303 survived to be transferred to the *Cossack*, which departed soon after the last man came aboard.

The *Altmark* affair outraged the Germans, enraged the Norwegians, and electrified the English population. Churchill's verve had saved the British sailors from five years of captivity. At the same time, the Norwegian government strongly protested this violation of their neutrality. In the months to come, that nation's leadership became increasingly fixated on the threat of British intervention in Norway and would ultimately be blindsided by the German invasion.

Below decks, *Cossack*'s boarding party rescued more than three hundred British merchant sailors who had been captured by *Graf Spee* during her depredations in the South Atlantic.

The launching ceremony for the pocket battleship *Admiral Scheer* on April Fools' Day, 1933. She and her *Deutschland*-class ships carried powerful 11-inch guns along with a secondary battery of eight 5.9-inch guns and eight torpedo tubes. She could outfight any heavy cruiser in the world.

encountered the armed merchant cruiser *Rawalpindi*. A converted passenger liner with minimal armor and a few 6-inch guns, the British vessel could neither fight effectively nor run away. As two of the most powerful warships afloat bore down on his ship, *Rawalpindi*'s skipper, Capt. E. C. Kennedy, refused a German request to surrender. His crew heard him say, "We'll fight them both. They'll sink us. And that will be that. Goodbye."

The Germans unleashed their broadsides, and the *Rawalpindi* endured a storm of 11-inch and 5.9-inch shellfire. An 11-inch shell hit the *Rawalpindi*'s forward magazine and touched off an explosion that split the ship in two. Two hundred thirty-eight members of her crew died, including her captain. Fewer than forty people survived.

Rawalpindi's sacrifice alerted the Admiralty to the new German threat, and the Home Fleet mobilized for action. Realizing their mission had been compromised, the Germans raced for home to try another day.

Meanwhile, *Graf Spee* sank three more Allied merchant ships. Two went down along the African coast. The third was sunk on December 7, 1939, while heading for South American waters. Documents recovered from that vessel showed the Germans that the mouth of the River Plate was a major British shipping hub. Langsdorff set a course for that fertile hunting ground.

Graf Spee had been operating at sea since August 21, 1939. Her engines, already in need of an overhaul before the outbreak of the war, were starting to suffer serious mechanical problems that reduced her speed to only twenty-three knots—barely faster than Britain's World War I–era R-class battleships. Should Langsdorff encounter one of the hunting groups searching for *Graf Spee*, he would not have the speed to escape.

Commodore Henry Harwood commanded Force G, one of the hunting groups operating in the South Atlantic. Composed of the heavy cruisers *Exeter* and *Cumberland* and light cruisers *Ajax* and *Achilles*, Force G

Launched in 1930, the *Koeln* was a *Koenigsberg*-class light cruiser whose service was hampered by structural weaknesses and a heavy fuel consumption rate that limited her radius of action. In 1940, she took part in the Norwegian campaign, but after that she was relegated to training and mine-laying duties.

was patrolling north of the Falkland Islands in early December. Harwood concluded that Langsdorff's next move would be against the shipping lanes flowing out of the River Plate. He ordered Force G to concentrate to the south of that area (minus the *Cumberland*, which was in the Falklands) and prepare for battle.

Harwood's intuition paid dividends when his force stumbled across *Graf Spee* shortly before 0600 on December 13, 1939. Langsdorff's Arado 196 had suffered engine failure, and without her scout plane in the air, *Graf Spee* was vulnerable to a surprise attack by the faster British cruisers. When his lookouts first spotted the British, he turned toward them and prepared to fight. Moments later, the full tactical picture came into

focus: the *Graf Spee* faced three capable ships, all of which were faster than his. Langsdorff has been criticized for not following standing orders and evading the British warships, but he didn't really have a choice. If he had tried to run, the cruisers would have chased him down. Some historians have suggested he could have tried to stay out of 6- and 8-inch gun range for as long as possible, using his 11-inch guns to hammer the British while he fled. But if he had turned his stern toward the enemy, he would have only been able to use the three 11-inch guns in the aft turret. Using half his available gun power would have made accurate fire control more difficult and probably would not have produced good results.

Admiral Raeder (lead row, second from right) walks shoulder to shoulder with the commander of the army, Reichswehrminister General von Blomberg (on Raeder's left), during a ceremonial review prior to the launching of *Admiral Scheer*.

Run or stand—either way, Langsdorff was in for a fight. Harwood had prepared for this moment and his captains had been drilled in the tactics they would use should they encounter the pocket battleship. *Exeter* would operate independently to hit the *Graf Spee* from one side while the two 6-inch gun cruisers operated as an integrated division and hit her from the other.

Graf Spee concentrated her fire on HMS *Exeter*. With full six-gun salvoes, it did not take long for the Germans to find the range. Their third attempt straddled the British cruiser, flaying the decks with steel splinters that killed the starboard torpedo crew and destroyed

Exeter's two Walrus floatplanes. The *Exeter* fired back, the gun crews working amid swirls of smoke and steam in their cramped and sweltering turrets. *Exeter* scored three direct hits before an 11-inch shell struck the B turret. The cataclysmic blast killed most of the men inside and sent a hurricane of shrapnel through the bridge that felled everyone but *Exeter*'s skipper. Wounded in the face, Capt. F. S. Bell made his way aft to the secondary con to continue the fight.

Despite the damage and two more 11-inch hits, *Exeter* executed a full-speed torpedo attack. *Graf Spee* briefly switched its main guns to the light cruisers before

Above: Deutschland on maneuvers in the North Sea. When the war began, she commenced raiding operations in the Atlantic. After capturing SS *City of Flint* and sinking two other vessels, she returned to Germany for a major refit. She was renamed *Luetzow* in 1940. *Opposite left:* The battle cruiser *Scharnhorst* saw extensive service in the war's early months, and her 11-inch guns sank such famous Royal Navy vessels as the HMS *Rawalpindi* and aircraft carrier HMS *Glorious*. *Opposite right::* The pocket battleship *Graf Spee* in southern Spain during the Civil War in 1937. *Graf Spee* first saw service on nonintervention patrols off the coast of Spain in support of Franco's Nationalist forces.

swinging them back to deliver another hammer blow to the *Exeter*. Two more main gun rounds knocked out the A turret and sparked a serious fire amidships. Another shell tore open her hull, causing a seven-degree list. With only one turret in action, Captain Bell refused to disengage.

Meanwhile, the two 6-inch cruisers sprinted forward in hopes of closing the range with *Graf Spee*. *Ajax* paid for her aggressiveness when an 11-inch shell struck the waterline beneath the X turret and penetrated the handling room. The explosion blew men to pieces;

rescue crews later found bloodied limbs embedded in the bulkheads.

That one hit knocked out both X and Y turrets, crippling *Ajax*'s firepower. Nevertheless, the ship stayed in the fight, its remaining batteries barking away at *Graf Spee*. Later, a hoist failed in B turret, reducing *Ajax* to three 6-inch guns. In the final moments of the battle, *Graf Spee* scored another hit on *Ajax* that tore away her top mast, dragging with it her radio antennae.

The running engagement lasted until 0740 when (continued on page 43)

Above: The predecessor of the Arado Ar-196 was the Heinkel He-60, a slow and vulnerable biplane whose service during World War II was relegated to short-range patrols over the Baltic. *Right:* An Arado 196 on patrol. *Opposite top:* A Royal Navy sailor waves his hat as a destroyer edges out of port. The British began the war with a significant shortage of destroyers and other escorts. *Opposite bottom:* The German pocket battleships were built for speed and gun power, making them dangerous opponents. They were well suited for their commerce-raiding mission, as they could outfight anything smaller and outrun anything larger than they were.

Above: The German navy's operating area included some of the roughest seas in the world. For the most part, the surface fleet was composed of well-built ships that functioned well in dismal conditions. *Below:* With the pocket battleships raiding the Atlantic, the Royal Navy devoted considerable fleet assets to escorting convoys. This stretched the already overcommitted surface fleet ever thinner, something that Admiral Raeder had counted on.

Graf Spee wrought havoc on the shipping lanes in the South Atlantic and Indian Ocean in 1939. Her skipper, Kapitän Hans Langsdorff, was a cagey officer who drove the British mad with his wily tactics. Under his command, *Graf Spee* became Germany's most successful pocket battleship, sinking fifty thousand tons of Allied shipping during its rampage through the South Atlantic.

(continued from page 39)
Hardwood broke off the fight. *Exeter* was a cripple by this point. Her last operational turret flooded out at 0730, making her all but useless. Her shattered decks were littered with sixty-one dead and twenty-three wounded.

Though the *Exeter* was badly shot up by the German raider, Harwood ordered his light cruisers to shadow *Graf Spee* and reported all her movements. *Exeter* turned for the naval base in the Falklands, while HMS *Cumberland* sped north to join in the chase.

Langsdorff was in a tight spot now. Ships from hunting groups all over the Atlantic were converging on him. He lacked the speed to outrun Harwood's cruisers, and his ship had suffered extensive damage in the fight. The British scored three 8-inch hits and seventeen 6-inch strikes, killing thirty-six men and wounding another fifty-nine.

The three 8-inch hits had done devastating damage. The first one destroyed the *Graf Spee*'s boiler room that generated the steam needed to move and clean raw fuel oil from the bunkers to the day tanks. Without this system functioning, the pocket battleship was reduced to about sixteen hours worth of available fuel. It could not be repaired at sea. The other two 8-inch strikes destroyed the ship's water purification plant and penetrated *Graf Spee*'s main belt armor.

One of the *Graf Spee*'s victims heads for the bottom.

The 6-inch shell hits had left a large hole in her bow and destroyed the ship's bakery and galley. The hit in the bow would slow her down even more and make her hard to handle in rough seas. No doubt, she would ship additional water in such conditions.

Langsdorff couldn't run away. Even if he could outrun Force G, he had less than a day's worth of useable fuel aboard. Escaping back to Germany was not an option.

He couldn't stand and fight either. His 11-inch ammunition stocks had been depleted in the fight with Harwood. Now, *Graf Spee* had only enough main gun rounds for about a half an hour of fighting.

Langsdorff could surrender. He could go down fighting and sacrifice his crew. Or he could try to reach a safe harbor, make repairs, and try to break out for home later.

Langsdorff chose to steam for the nearest neutral port, which was Montevideo up the River Plate. *Graf Spee*

Graf Spee's crew watches another Allied cargo ship roll over and sink while standing in the shadow of their ship's Arado 196 scout plane.

A Saro London flying boat. Thirty-one of these awkward-looking patrol planes were constructed during the 1930s. Three units—201 Squadron in Scotland, 202 Squadron at Gibraltar, and 240 Squadron at Invergordon, Scotland—flew antisubmarine patrols with their Londons until 1940 and 1941 when they were finally replaced by Sunderlands and American-built Lockheed Hudsons. They had a range of about a thousand miles and could carry two thousand pounds of bombs, mines, or depth charges.

Above: Deutschland returns to Germany. During the Spanish Civil War, she was bombed by Republican aircraft; nearly a hundred of her crew were killed or wounded in the attack. *Below:* HMS *Exeter*'s final moments. After crippling *Graf Spee*, she served in the Dutch East Indies campaign, where Japanese cruisers sank her. This photo, taken from a Japanese plane, was taken only minutes before she slid beneath the waves.

Graf Spee burns after Langsdorff scuttled her outside Montevideo Harbor.

reached the port just before midnight on the thirteenth. Her arrival unleashed a storm of diplomatic intrigue and debate. Ultimately, the Uruguayan government allowed *Graf Spee* to stay for only seventy-two hours. This wasn't enough time for the crew to make their crippled warship ready for the long voyage home. At the same time, a British counter-intelligence operation convinced Langsdorff that a large force had assembled off the River Plate.

Rather than sacrifice his crew, Langsdorff chose to scuttle *Graf Spee* in the Plate River estuary. Two days later, he wrapped himself in an Imperial German naval ensign and shot himself. His crew was interned in Argentina, where most of them remained after the war.

Though the Kriegsmarine, Hitler, and history have judged Langsdorff harshly, Captain Langsdorff faced a no-win situation. He chose the only noble path: protect the lives of his men. This is not surprising. Langsdorff's compassion had been the hallmark of his tenure at sea. Though *Graf Spee* captured or sank nine Allied merchant ships, not a single merchant mariner had been killed by the German vessel. Langsdorff showed mercy and scrupulously cared for the prisoners his men took during those engagements.

His suicide served as an act of atonement for the loss of his warship. In the long and brutal campaign in the Atlantic, it is hard to find a more tragic figure than Hans Langsdorff.

CHAPTER THREE

THE IRON ROAD

Lieutenant Commander Jan Grudzinski peered through the submarine *Orzel*'s periscope and through the heavy seas could just see a ship on the horizon.

Grudzinski identified it as a German passenger liner. *Orzel* was operating off the Norwegian coast near Lillesand. This seemed an odd place to encounter a German liner, especially since she was heading north on a course that would take her to Bergen.

She was a legitimate target—the first one *Orzel* had encountered since the war began. Grudzinski reduced speed from seven to three knots and waited for the German liner to come into range.

Grudzinski had spent his adult life in the Polish navy. In 1939, *Orzel* sortied into the Baltic with orders to hunt for German ships. Instead, her skipper sailed to Tallinn, where the Estonians interned the sub and her crew. The skipper abandoned his men and turned command over to Grudzinski, who had only joined *Orzel*'s complement three months before after spending the 1930s aboard mine sweepers. Grudzinski was an unknown quantity to the crew, who weren't sure he was any more trustworthy than their skipper.

Whatever doubts the crew had about him vanished when Grudzinski told them they were going to escape. In the dead of night, the Poles overpowered the two guards aboard *Orzel* and steamed into the Baltic Sea. After dropping off the Estonian guards on a Swedish island, Grudzinski sailed *Orzel* to Great Britain, where the ship's daring escape earned headlines. They were toasted and feted; Grudzinski even spent time with King George the VI.

Now, on their eighth patrol, they finally had a chance to strike back at the Germans. After stalking the liner for over an hour, Grudzinski identified her as the 5,261-ton *Rio de Janeiro*.

The Royal Navy was not conducting an unrestricted submarine war against Germany in the winter of 1940, so the Poles could not just blow the *Rio* out of the water. Instead, Grudzinski ordered his boat to the surface. When *Orzel*'s bow crested the mountainous swells, the German liner tried to bolt for Norwegian territorial water. Grudzinski gave chase. *Orzel* was Dutch-built and capable of twenty knots. The *Rio* had no hope of evading the Poles. Grudzinski ordered the ship to stop its engines and send the ship's master across with the

Opposite: The Polish submarine *Orzel* became legendary at the start of World War II. After making an epic escape from the Baltic, her crew joined up with the Royal Navy and fearlessly patrolled the North Sea. It was *Orzel*'s crew that detected the impending German amphibious assault on Norway.

German troops prepare to load up into a cargo ship for the run to Norway in April 1940.

Rio's cargo manifest. The Germans acknowledged the order only after Grudzinski punctuated with a burst of machine gunfire.

As the seas raged, *Rio de Janeiro* lowered a small boat. The men aboard pretended to row toward *Orzel*, but it became obvious they had no intent of actually complying with Grudzinski's order. Then *Orzel*'s radioman reported that the *Rio* was transmitting in code. Grudzinski decided enough was enough. He gave the Germans five minutes to abandon ship.

The Germans didn't react. *Orzel* fired a single torpedo, which missed. Grudzinksi launched a second. This one caught the *Rio* amidships. The explosion tore a hole in her hull, and the liner developed a starboard list.

German soldiers suddenly appeared on deck running pell-mell in all directions. Some jumped over the side. Others threw bits of debris into the water, hoping to use

them as flotation devices. Strangely, nobody tried to get the lifeboats lowered.

Orzel circled the *Rio* and put a torpedo into her port side. The fish broke the liner's back and she sank within minutes. The water filled with dead and dying German soldiers.

Two Norwegian patrol boats had arrived during the initial standoff; now they steamed in to rescue the *Rio de Janeiro*'s survivors. The Germans they fished out of the frigid North Sea told a curious tale to their rescuers. A few explained that they were en route to Bergen to protect Norway, at the request of the Norwegian government, from an invading British force. The Norwegian navy reported this, but the government failed to understand the meaning of this intelligence. Fearful of an invasion by the Allies, the Norwegian government was blind to a possible attack from Germany.

Above: The light cruiser *Koeln* belonged to Group 3, the invasion force tasked with capturing Bergen, Norway. She and the *Koenigsberg* escorted the transport *Karl Peters* into the Norwegian port, where a thousand German troops were successfully landed. The *Koenigsberg* was sunk a short time later by Fleet Air Arm Skua dive bombers. *Below: Emden* took part in the attack on Oslo, Norway, in April 1940 with Group 5. During the fight up Oslofjord, the cruiser *Bluecher* was sunk by coastal defense guns. After Oslo fell, *Emden* was used as a communication and control ship until the end of the campaign.

Above: The French cruiser *Duquesne* (seen here in lead formation) took part in the pursuit of the *Graf Spee* and then ended up in Alexandria, Egypt, in 1940. The French fleet played only a small role in the Norwegian campaign and accomplished little during the first nine months of the war. *Below:* The Germans sent shock troops aboard Junkers Ju-52 transports to capture important Norwegian airfields at the outset of the campaign.

Almost the entire German fleet was committed to the Norwegian invasion. Here, a formation of German minelayers steams through the North Sea.

Orzel had fired the opening shots of one of the most unusual campaigns of World War II—the struggle for Norway. It was a campaign that would have direct consequences on the battle of the Atlantic for years to come.

The Germans needed Swedish iron ore to sustain the Reich's war machine. In 1938, Germany imported twenty-two million tons of iron ore. Nine million came from Sweden. Another nine and a half million came from countries cut off from the Third Reich by the British naval blockade, making the Swedish mines in the northern Kiruna and Gallivare areas all the more vital to German industry.

The ore left these mines via a single rail line that ran to Lulea, a Swedish port that was only open during the spring and summer. In the winter, the Swedes freighted the ore to Narvik, Norway, which remained open year-round. From there, the Germans ran convoys

of cargo ships down between the Norwegian coast and the outlaying islands. That narrow stretch of Norwegian territorial waters became known as the Iron Road.

When Winston Churchill returned to the Admiralty, he sought to close the Iron Road, either by sending an Anglo-French expeditionary force to capture Narvik or through mining operations. Prime Minister Neville Chamberlain's government couldn't decide if it would initiate such a plan until it was too late. Both the Norwegians and the Germans picked up on the possibility of an Allied move in Norway. Alarmed, the Nazis planned a daring campaign to seize Norway and secure the flow of iron ore to the Reich's factories.

To pull off such an operation without command of the North Sea required surprise and considerable air power. Using most of their navy, the Germans planned to land assault troops at six key ports. Two waves of water-borne reinforcements would sustain those

German airborne forces captured key airfields, bridges, and bases in the spring of 1940 in the first combat jumps of World War II.

soldiers. Meanwhile, airborne troops would seize key installations in southern Norway, including the airfield complex at Stavanger.

The intricate plan demanded precise timing from a lot of moving parts. The naval elements left ports around Germany and even Russia starting on April 3, 1940. The first assault waves were to strike simultaneously at 0500 April 9.

As German ships steamed for Narvik, Trondheim, Bergen, Stavanger, Christiansand, and Olso, the British government finally approved a mining operation along the Iron Road. A Royal Navy task force sortied in early April to lay the mines.

HMS *Glowworm* was one of the destroyers sent to screen the mining effort. A modern G-class destroyer, *Glowworm* was armed with four 4.7-inch guns and ten torpedo tubes. On the morning of April 8, after spending much of the previous day in a howling North Sea storm

in search of a sailor washed overboard, *Glowworm* encountered the German destroyer *Z-11 Bernd von Arnim*. In towering seas, the two vessels fought a running battle for several moments as *Z-11*, laden with troops bound for Trondheim, sought to escape the spirited British warship. A second German destroyer joined the fight, but Lt. Cmdr. Gerard Broadmead Roope, *Glowworm*'s skipper, refused to leave the fight. The German destroyers called for help, then led *Glowworm* right into the path of the 8-inch gun cruiser *Admiral Hipper*. With heavy shells raining down, Roope turned *Glowworm* directly for the ten thousand–ton German warship and rammed her. The collision tore open *Hipper*'s hull and caused her to ship some five hundred tons of water.

Glowworm suffered crippling damage in the collision. Four hundred yards from *Hipper*, she was smothered by gunfire until *Glowworm* rolled over and sank stern first.

The North Sea weather played havoc on both sides during the Norwegian campaign, leading to many missed opportunities and narrow escapes.

Roope and 110 of his men went down with their ship. *Hipper*'s crew plucked thirty-nine oil-soaked, freezing survivors from the windblown seas.

Later, *Hipper*'s captain, Helmuth Heye, sent a letter via the Red Cross to the British recommending Roope for the Victoria Cross. His gesture was the only time an enemy combatant has made such a recommendation. It was approved, and Roope's family later received his posthumous VC.

That night, with the German task forces right off shore, the Norwegian government still failed to take emergency defensive measures. A partial mobilization was agreed to, but instead of using the radio waves to rally the reservists, the government decided to mail notices to its servicemen. Though the word of *Rio de Janeiro*'s destination had also reached Oslo, the government elected not to take measures to protect the country's coastal cities.

The next morning, as the German invasion began, the battlecruisers *Scharnhorst* and *Gneisenau* plowed through a fierce northwesterly gale off Narvik. The Narvik attack force had the farthest to travel, which exposed its swift destroyers to the Royal Navy longer than any other element in the operation, hence the heavy escort.

Around 0600 on April 9, as the destroyers steamed into Narvik, the British battleship HMS *Renown*, which had been screening Britain's mining operation, detected *Scharnhorst* and *Gneisenau* on her radar. From eleven thousand yards, the capital ships fired salvoes at each other as they crashed through the enormous swells. *Scharnhorst* had already suffered some structural damage as a result of the weather. Now, as the two sides grappled in poor visibility, her radar malfunctioned, effectively blinding her for the rest of the engagement.

Cruiser *Koenigsberg* fell victim to Fleet Air Arm dive bombers in the first sinking by air attack of a major warship in military history.

The German captains remained under Raeder's general order to avoid combat with the Royal Navy whenever possible. As the *Renown*'s 15-inch shells rained down around them, the battle cruisers tried to flee northward. Before they made good their escape, *Renown* scored two hits on *Gneisenau*. One put her main optical fire control system out of action. The other took out one of her turrets.

During the chase, the heavy seas battered the German ships. Green water poured over their bows as the ships crashed down into the troughs between the titanic waves. Aboard the *Scharnhorst*, flooding shorted out the ammunition hoist for the forward main turret, knocking it out of action. The violence of the gale also damaged her starboard turbine, reducing her speed significantly. Nevertheless, the weather helped the German ships escape. They sailed into the Arctic Sea where they hid for several days before slipping back to Germany.

Meanwhile, the German task forces launched their near-simultaneous surprise assaults on the six Norwegian ports. Protected by outdated forts armed with nineteenth-century cannon, the cities did not hold out for long, though the forts did inflict heavy losses on the invaders. Near Oslo, Fort Oscarborg waited to fire on the heavy cruiser *Bluecher* until she was just a few hundred yards away as she steamed through the fjord leading to the Norwegian capital. The sudden blast from the fort's ancient 280mm guns tore the heavy cruiser apart. Two torpedoes fired from the fort finished her off. She sank with the loss more than a thousand men.

Elsewhere, the Norwegian defenders damaged several other German warships, including the pocket battleship *Luetzow* and the heavy cruiser *Koenigsberg*. *Luetzow* was nearly lost two days later as she sailed back for Germany when a British submarine torpedoed her. The attack destroyed her rudder and propellers, and she had

Above: German troops take cover during an air attack in southern Norway. Though the initial assault succeeded wildly, the campaign lasted for months and was a hard-fought, pitched affair that inflicted heavy losses on both sides. *Right:* A German sailor stands watch over a wreath dropped to honor the men who died aboard *Bluecher.* About a thousand men died when the ship was sunk by Norwegian coastal defenses. The wreck leaked oil for decades, finally prompting the Norwegians to hire a company to extract as much as possible to prevent environmental damage. The oil was actually sold after it had been recovered in 1994. One of the ship's Arado 196 scout planes was also salvaged and is currently in a Norwegian air museum.

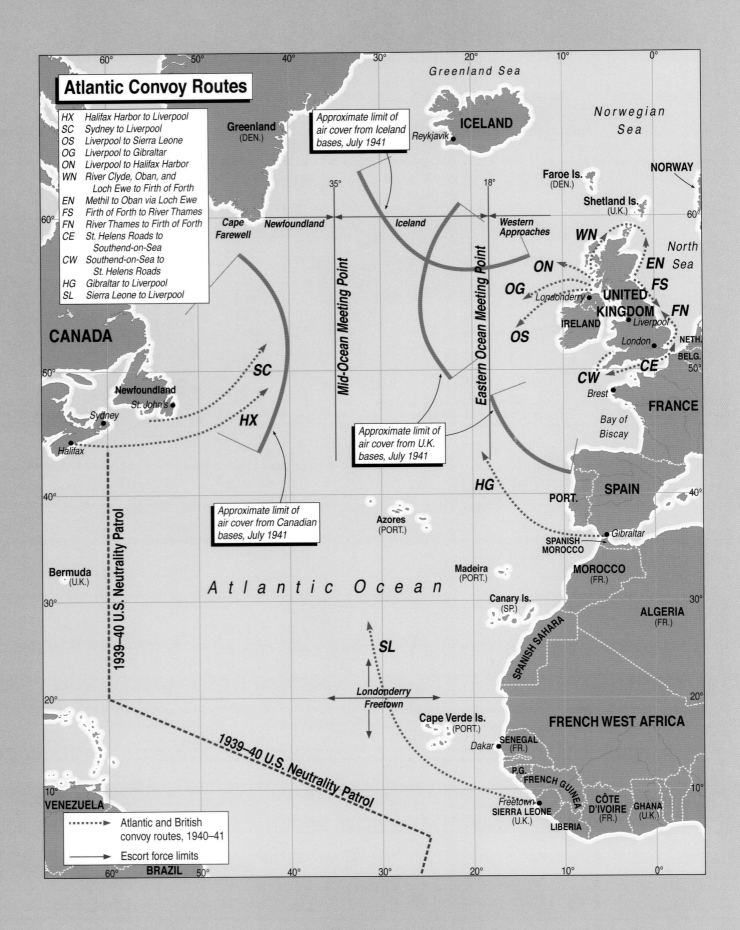

Atlantic Convoy Routes

HX   Halifax Harbor to Liverpool
SC   Sydney to Liverpool
OS   Liverpool to Sierra Leone
OG   Liverpool to Gibraltar
ON   Liverpool to Halifax Harbor
WN   River Clyde, Oban, and
        Loch Ewe to Firth of Forth
EN   Methil to Oban via Loch Ewe
FS   Firth of Forth to River Thames
FN   River Thames to Firth of Forth
CE   St. Helens Roads to
        Southend-on-Sea
CW   Southend-on-Sea to
        St. Helens Roads
HG   Gibraltar to Liverpool
SL   Sierra Leone to Liverpool

Approximate limit of air cover from Iceland bases, July 1941

Approximate limit of air cover from U.K. bases, July 1941

Approximate limit of air cover from Canadian bases, July 1941

Mid-Ocean Meeting Point

Eastern Ocean Meeting Point

1939–40 U.S. Neutrality Patrol

Greenland Sea

Norwegian Sea

ICELAND
Reykjavik

Greenland (DEN.)

Cape Farewell

Newfoundland

Iceland

Western Approaches

Faroe Is. (DEN.)

Shetland Is. (U.K.)

NORWAY

North Sea

WN
EN
ON
FS
OG
FN
OS
CE
CW

Londonderry
UNITED KINGDOM
IRELAND
Liverpool
London

NETH.
BELG.

CANADA

Newfoundland
St. John's
Sydney
Halifax

SC

HX

Brest

FRANCE

Bay of Biscay

HG

SPAIN
PORT.

Atlantic Ocean

Azores (PORT.)

Bermuda (U.K.)

Madeira (PORT.)

Canary Is. (SP.)

SPANISH MOROCCO
Gibraltar

MOROCCO (FR.)

ALGERIA (FR.)

SPANISH SAHARA

SL

Londonderry
Freetown

Cape Verde Is. (PORT.)

FRENCH WEST AFRICA

Dakar
SENEGAL (FR.)

P.G.
FRENCH GUINEA

VENEZUELA

Freetown
SIERRA LEONE (U.K.)
LIBERIA

CÔTE D'IVOIRE (FR.)

GHANA (U.K.)

1939–40 U.S. Neutrality Patrol

BRAZIL

- - - - ▶ Atlantic and British
             convoy routes, 1940–41

———▶ Escort force limits

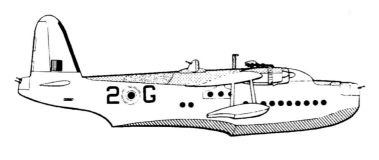

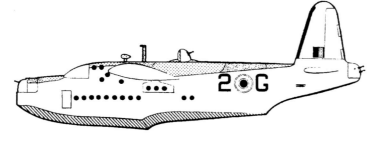

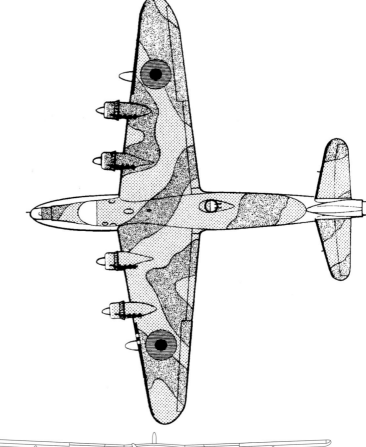

Above and right: The Short Sunderland flying boat became a key part of British anti-submarine strategy. While serving as a patrol bomber, it was also effective for sea rescues. *The-Blueprints.com*

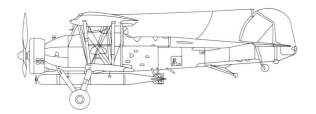

The Fairey Swordfish torpedo bomber was already outdated at the start of the war, but nevertheless served admirably, eventually playing a role in the sinking of the *Bismarck*. *The-Blueprints.com*

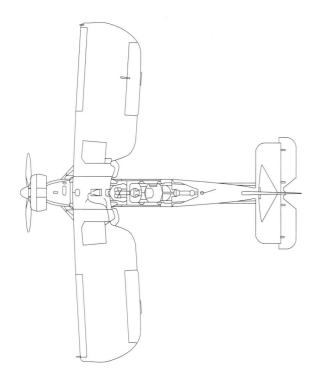

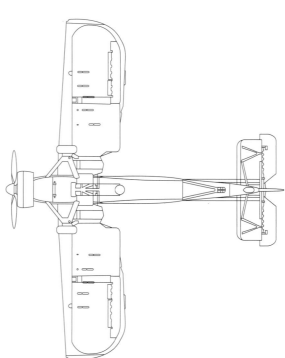

Above: A wartime German watercolor of the fleet in action during the Norway campaign. *Opposite top:* Two German destroyers prowling the seas. The Norwegian campaign saw one of the few destroyer-on-destroyer actions between the German and Royal navies. *Opposite bottom:* A German destroyer in a Norwegian fjord. The Battle of Narvik cost the German destroyer flotillas greatly.

to be towed to Kiel, where she was out of action for the rest of the year.

On the evening of the ninth, the submarine HMS *Truant* caught the light cruiser *Karlsruhe* with a long-range torpedo salvo. She suffered such heavy damage that her crew was forced to scuttle her.

Despite these setbacks, the Kriegsmarine still accomplished its missions. By nightfall, the troops embarked on its warships had captured almost every objective. The Norwegian army, thrown into disarray by the surprise attack, was all but overwhelmed.

The initial success came at an increasingly steep price as the Allies reacted to the German invasion. The

next morning, a flight of Fleet Air Arm Blackburn Skua dive bombers found the *Koenigsberg* tied up to the mole in Bergen Harbor. The Skua crews sent her to the bottom with a masterful dive-bombing attack. The *Koenigsberg* became the first major warship to be sunk by aircraft in World War II.

Earlier that morning, the British counterattacked the German force in Narvik Harbor with a five-ship destroyer task force. Led by Captain Warburton-Lee, the tin cans slipped into Ofotfjord below Narvik undetected. At 0430, masked by a spring snow squall, the British surprised the German ships riding at anchor. The British sank several cargo vessels full of

The aftermath at Narvik.

ammunition and equipment for the two thousand troops that had come ashore on the ninth. They also sank two of the ten German destroyers there before withdrawing virtually unscathed.

Once outside the Ofotfjord, Warburton-Lee had two options. He could have stayed put and blockaded the approach to Narvik and waited for the battleship *Warspite* and her nine destroyers. That task force was close at hand, and uniting with it surely would have crushed the remaining German naval forces. The other option was to go back in and finish the job right away.

He returned to Narvik, etching another page in the Royal Navy's long tradition of aggressiveness. Unfortunately, Warburton-Lee acted on faulty intelligence. Local Norwegians had told him that there were only six German destroyers around Narvik. Figuring he'd knocked two out and damaged several more, the loss of surprise did not seem like a major issue to him. The odds had been reduced.

He actually faced eight destroyers, now alerted, though short on fuel. In the narrow waters of the fjord, flanked by towering snow-capped cliffs, the British destroyers steamed directly into a trap. From inlets and side fjords, the German vessels poured into the main channel, boxing the British in. A point-blank duel broke out. Warburton-Lee's flagship, HMS *Hardy*, took a direct hit in the bridge that killed him early in the fight. HMS *Hunter*, pounded by 5.9-inch shells and set ablaze, collided with *Hotspur*, which had also been damaged. *Hotspur* managed to escape into open water, but *Hunter* sank in the fjord and *Hardy* had to be beached. The two remaining British destroyers withdrew out of the fjord, but not before sinking an ammunition ship.

A German antiaircraft machine gunner protects shipping in Norway during the 1940 campaign.

The morning cost the British two destroyers sunk, one seriously damaged. In return, Warburton-Lee's sailors gave a tremendous account of themselves, sinking two destroyers and damaging five more while taking out six supply ships whose holds contained vital supplies for the troops ashore. For his actions that morning, Warburton-Lee became World War II's first recipient of the Victoria Cross.

On April 12, *Warspite* and nine destroyers sailed into Ofotfjord and wiped out the remaining German vessels at Narvik. The Kriegsmarine lost almost half of its available destroyers in the bid to capture this vital far north port.

Over the next month, the British and French navies supported landing operations along the Norwegian coast. Though the Kriegsmarine virtually vanished from the campaign after Narvik, the Luftwaffe picked up the slack, deploying almost 750 to Norway.

With command of the air, the Germans gained control over the situation and the Allies were forced to evacuate their surviving men. The Allied troops in Central Norway were pulled out in the teeth of heavy Luftwaffe opposition. German bombers sank two destroyers during desperate fighting at Namsos Harbor.

That left a force of about twenty-four thousand French, British, and Polish troops around Narvik. The outnumbered German garrison there was finally driven out on May 28. The victory proved short-lived. A few days later, the Allies withdrew from this final Norwegian foothold as France herself was imperiled by German invasion.

The Kriegsmarine sortied again in hopes of striking at the shipping in the Narvik area. *Gneisenau* and *Scharnhorst* formed the core of this force, which also included *Hipper* and three destroyers.

THE SHIPS THAT SAVED THE CAUSE

In the spring of 1940, as Norway succumbed to the German onslaught, the Royal Navy evacuated King Haakon VII and his government. Established in London, the Norwegian government in exile possessed an ace in the hole that played a crucial role in the Atlantic. In 1939, though Norway's population barely topped three million people, the country boasted the world's fourth-largest merchant marine force. With a thousand modern vessels, the Norwegians could haul more cargo than just about any other nation. Want oil moved across the Atlantic? Call the Norwegians. Their fleet included a whopping 20 percent of the world's oil tankers.

When King Haakon reached London, he delivered the 4.8 million–ton Norwegian merchant marine to the Allied cause. Great Britain's survival depended on those ships. By 1942, 40 percent of Britain's oil reached the Home Islands aboard Norwegian tankers. Yet, the Norwegian crews never received credit for this crucial component to the Allied victory.

The price paid to keep Britain in the war was a steep one. U-boats, mines, and the Luftwaffe destroyed fully half of the Norwegian merchant fleet. These five hundred ships took three thousand unheralded, heroic men down with them.

Though the German conquest of Norway seemed at the time to be a stunning victory, there was a hidden dimension the Third Reich never envisioned. The Nazi invasion in the north ultimately delivered to the British the very means of their salvation.

Above: British destroyers scored some of the few Allied victories in Norway during the 1940 campaign. Their actions at Narvik reflected great credit on the Royal Navy and its tradition of engaging the enemy more closely. *Opposite:* The Royal Navy battleship *Nelson* was among the most modern ships in the British fleet in 1940.

As the last of the troops withdrew from Norway, the small RAF force defending Narvik tried to escape as well. The British needed every aircraft for the coming struggle for the Home Isles so the decision was made to try to land ten Gloster Gladiators and eight Hawker Hurricanes onto the carrier *Glorious*. The RAF pilots had never landed on a carrier before, nor were their aircraft equipped with arrestor hooks. Nevertheless, all eighteen got aboard *Glorious*'s pitching deck.

The next morning, *Glorious* steamed for home at a sedate seventeen knots with only twelve of her seventeen boilers lit. Captain D'Orly Hughes had only come to the carrier arm ten months before following a career in the submarine branch. His ignorance of carrier operations created friction with his air commander, Capt. J. B. Heath. After a raging fight erupted between the two men, D'Orly Hughes dumped Heath at Scapa Flow, intending to court martial him for cowardice in combat.

On June 8, D'Orly Hughes had no combat air patrol overhead, no air searches out scouting for enemy ships,

and no aircraft spotted on the flight deck. The air group remained in *Glorious*'s hangar with some of its aircraft at ten minutes' notice. Worst of all, the screen for the *Glorious* consisted of only two destroyers. For a capital ship, one of a half-dozen left to the Royal Navy, to be so lightly guarded in the spring of 1940 was utter negligence. Such folly—a repeat of the loss of the HMS *Courageous*—would cost the lives of good and devoted men once again.

At 1600, *Gneisenau* and *Scharnhorst* surprised the three ship task force. Destroyers *Ardent* and *Acasta* sacrificed themselves in a desperate bid to save *Glorious*. Both went down with the loss of almost everyone aboard. Their crews died in vain, as *Glorious* was not spared. Unable to run away, unable to fight, she was battered by 11-inch shell hits, one of which killed everyone on the bridge. Fires started on the hangar deck, power was lost, and the ship began to list to starboard.

Glorious went down, blazing bow to stern, only a few minutes later. Less than 50 men survived out of

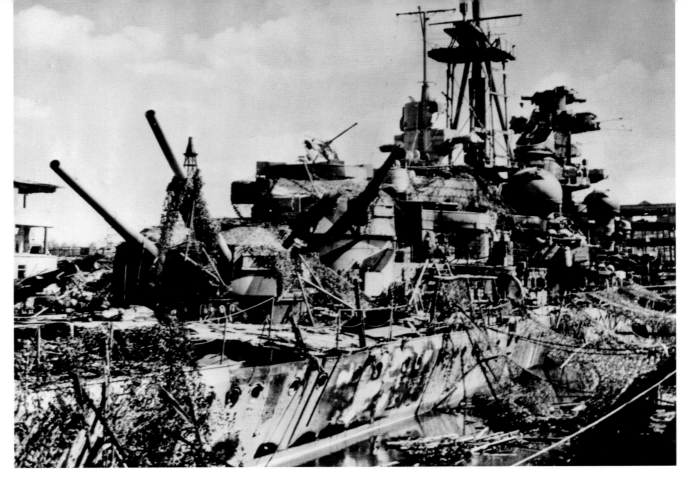

Above: The German navy lost a significant percentage of its operational strength during the Norwegian campaign—so much so that it was never able to undertake such a large-scale operation again. Many of the fleet's most important warships had either been sunk or severely damaged. *Right:* A British destroyer as seen from a German torpedo boat during a skirmish in the North Sea.

Royal Navy destroyers in action off the coast of Norway.

the almost 1,500 aboard the three British ships. Not a single one of the RAF pilots who bravely landed aboard the day before were among the pitiful few to be rescued.

The disaster left the British Fleet Air Arm with but five aircraft carriers. It would remain a slender reed for the rest of the war.

This last action concluded the Norwegian campaign. The Germans secured their supply of ore and could protect the Iron Road with the full might of the Luftwaffe. Additionally, the Germans gained air and naval bases closer to the Atlantic—and to the Arctic Sea—which would be used in the years ahead to launch operations against Allied convoys. The strategic gain in this regard made the campaign more than worthwhile to the German war effort.

At the same time, it came at a brutal cost to the Kriegsmarine. The victory all but wiped out Hitler's surface battle. Most of those vessels that survived had suffered damage that required months of yard time to repair. Without it, there was little chance of ending the war by direct invasion of England, even if the German Luftwaffe managed to win the Battle of Britain.

The undersea force did not suffer the same heavy losses, but their performance during the campaign was judged a failure. Admiral Raeder had deployed most of his operational subs to patrol the North Sea, where they accomplished little. The effort stripped the Atlantic of U-boats, and the British convoys there saw little enemy contact through the spring of 1940.

In April, the U-boats sank one supply ship, the British submarine *Thistle* and five merchant ships, the lowest monthly total of the war to date. Worse, there was no shortage of opportunities to inflict great damage on the Royal Navy. U-boats attacked *Warspite* on four separate occasions and launched torpedoes sixteen other times at British cruisers and destroyers. They also attacked transports heading to and from Norway ten other times.

On one memorable patrol, Gunther Prien, the "bull of Scapa Flow," took *U-47* into a fjord to launch a night surface attack on the Allied shipping riding at

A Stuka Geschwader on the ground in Norway. With Ju-87s overhead, Allied troops and ships came under constant, accurate dive-bombing attacks.

anchor. Despite firing two full torpedo spreads at stationary targets, the Kriegsmarine's most famous U-boat skipper failed to sink a single vessel. Nearly every skipper reported such disastrous results. The crews grew convinced that they had been sent into battle with faulty torpedoes.

They were right. The torpedoes were designed to run below a targeted ship where the vessel's magnetic signature would trigger its detonator. This way, the weapon could maximize damage by exploding under the ship's unarmored keel. The theory behind the torpedo was sound. The engineering was not.

A hasty investigation in May discovered that the boats had been equipped with new four-bladed arming propellers for their torpedoes. Thanks to faulty

manufacture and a lack of testing, the new mechanisms failed about 10 percent of the time. Further study revealed that underwater deposits of iron ore often spoofed magnetic detonators. In the fjords, they proved useless, detonating prematurely or not at all. Above latitude 62 degrees, they malfunctioned so often that Doenitz declared that his men did not have a torpedo that could be used in northern seas.

The investigation discovered other problems as well. The torpedoes could be set to run at different depths so the crews could tailor their attacks to the size and draught of their target. Set the torpedo to the wrong depth, and it could run too deep to do any harm. Set it too shallow, and it would not run under the target as designed. At times the torpedoes would not run at the adjusted setting. The problem was so erratic and difficult to track down that it was not solved until January 1942. In fact, the Germans first detected the issue during the Spanish Civil War in 1938, but little was done to fix it.

These flaws forced the U-boats to use World War I–style contact detonators. To inflict damage, the subs had to physically hit the sides of their targets with their torpedoes. Yet this low-tech approach revealed another failure: the contact detonators would not work if the torpedo struck the target at certain angles.

As a stopgap, Doenitz ordered new contact detonators to be produced that were copies of the Royal Navy's design. The Germans had recently captured a crippled British submarine and had studied its torpedo technology. But it would be months before the new detonators were ready for fleet use. In the meantime, Doenitz issued byzantine guidelines for using the current torpedoes that were so complicated that he wrote in his war diary, "I would never give them to operational boats except in the present circumstances."

Later analysis concluded that during the Norway campaign, the faulty torpedoes cost the Kriegsmarine hits on the *Warspite*, seven Allied cruisers, and seven destroyers. Over the course of the war's first year, missed opportunities piled up, and more than one postwar historian has suggested that the failure of this critical piece of technology played a key role in Britain's ultimate salvation in 1940 and 1941. The problems were so numerous and so difficult to solve that the U-boat crews would not sail with fully functional torpedoes until early 1943. Doenitz later wrote, "I do not believe that ever in the history of war can soldiers have been sent out against the enemy with such a useless weapon."

Though the Norwegian campaign ended in the summer of 1940, the Norwegian resistance carried on with the fighting for five more years. Their guerrilla activities proved to be among the most successful against the Nazis during World War II, reflecting the indomitable nature of the Norwegian people.

CHAPTER FOUR

GLUECKLICHE

On May 10, 1940, the German army totally altered the balance of power in the North Atlantic. Before dawn, more than 115 divisions struck the Allied lines in Holland, Belgium, and France. The Anglo-French military leadership expected a repeat of the 1914 Schlieffen Plan, which saw the German army sweep through the Low Countries into Northern France. To counter it, the cream of the Allied ground forces swung like a gate north into Belgium to take up defensive positions behind rivers and canals. Refighting the last war never ends well, as the French learned. Again.

Forget Schlieffen. The Wehrmacht's Panzer divisions poured into the virtually unguarded Ardennes region of Belgium. Brushing aside light resistance, the Panzers split the Allied armies in half as they dashed through the Stenhay Gap into France and drove for the coast. The Allied troops in Belgium and Holland fell back to Dunkirk, while those that escaped to the south prepared to defend France proper.

By the end of the month, the four hundred thousand Allied soldiers around Dunkirk found themselves trapped against the North Sea as the Panzers waited for Hitler's orders to finish them off. Their only salvation

lay in the Royal Navy. The Admiralty threw together an evacuation plan, dubbed Operation Dynamo, that would send thirty-eight precious destroyers into the cauldron at Dunkirk. With the skies owned by the Luftwaffe, it was certain that ship losses at the hands of Stukas and Ju-88s would be great. Nevertheless, it had to be done. Along with the destroyers, the Royal Navy assembled about 850 vessels of every size and purpose to carry out the rescue effort.

From May 28 to June 4, these ships, which included civilian yachts and motorboats, pulled 338,000 men out of the Dunkirk pocket. The effort cost the British six of the thirty-eight destroyers committed to Dynamo, while another twenty-six were damaged.

This left the British with just seventy-four operational destroyers to protect the empire's waterways from Singapore to Nova Scotia. The Royal Navy was being stretched to the breaking point with little help on the horizon from England's backward shipyards.

Shortly after Dunkirk, Winston Churchill, now prime minister, asked President Franklin Roosevelt for a loan of some forty or fifty mothballed World War I–vintage American destroyers in order to boost the Royal

Opposite: At Dunkirk, the Royal Navy fought furiously against marauding Luftwaffe aircraft as the British Expeditionary Force was pulled off the beaches.

The German offensive in the west devastated the Allied armies. Here, a World War I—era French FT-17 tank lies on its side in the aftermath of desperate fighting in May 1940.

Navy until new construction efforts made good on the losses. Churchill needed those ships, but FDR was initially noncommittal.

Only six days after the Royal Navy completed the Dunkirk evacuation, Italy declared war on Great Britain. The sudden stroke altered the strategic balance at sea at a time when the French navy's future seemed uncertain at best. The Italian navy included four battleships (with two more almost complete), nineteen cruisers, fifty-two destroyers, and 110 submarines. The ships were well constructed and formidable technological weapons. The Mediterranean sea lanes that carried so much of Britain's fuel and oil from the Middle East to the Home Isles would no longer be safe. After June 10, 1940,

British convoys had to be routed around the Cape of Good Hope. The advantage of the Suez Canal had been erased by Mussolini's decision to enter the war.

The handful of remaining Royal Navy destroyers could not be everywhere at once. Escorting convoys, protecting the Home Fleet, and screening the task forces in the South Atlantic, Gibraltar, and Alexandria—as well as maintaining a presence in Asia at Singapore—simply became too great of a task for the diminished force. Worse, a new threat loomed.

France collapsed in the third week of June. Within days of the French surrender, the British faced a seaborne invasion for the first time since 1803. With the army's artillery and tanks lying abandoned on the battlefields

Left: Captured Allied soldiers march to POW-holding compounds in the shadow of an inbound Junkers Ju-52 transport in May 1940. *Below:* German assault troops cross a canal in the Low Countries. Both Holland and Belgium were soon overwhelmed and surrendered, though Free Dutch and Belgian units fought with the British until the war's end.

The Allies had no answer to the fast-moving German Panzer columns that shattered the lines in Northern France. Here a Panzer III medium tank negotiates a roadblock.

of Belgium and France, the defense of the Home Isles rested on the Royal Air Force and the Royal Navy.

Should invasion come, cruisers and destroyers would be the best warships to intercept the German amphibious flotillas, which would consist of barges and small craft. To prepare for that event, the Royal Navy stripped the Home Fleet and other commands of both types of ships and stationed them in ports around southern England to be ready at a moment's notice to repel any enemy force. At a time when their services were desperately needed elsewhere, half of the navy's remaining destroyers, plus six cruisers, ended up chained to the Channel coast for the summer and fall of 1940.

The redeployment denuded the North Atlantic convoys of most of its escorts right at the moment when

Doenitz sent his U-boats back into the fray. Five days after the invasion of Western Europe, the first German subs set sail for the Atlantic. They found the pickings ripe. England had never been more vulnerable.

With hardly more than two dozen U-boats, Doenitz's wolves sank fifty-eight ships (284,113 tons) in June alone. During July and August, ninety-two more went down, depriving the British of another 463,443 tons. With the British focused on the safety of the Home Isles, the U-boat force caused utter havoc in what became known as the Glueckliche, or "Happy Time."

When France surrendered, the British lost 20 percent of its overseas imports in one blow. Now, as shipping losses mounted in the Atlantic, the long-term ability to feed the nation dimmed. Yet, the short-term threat was

Above: French troops await their fate after being captured in the spring of 1940. *Below:* The aftermath at Dunkirk.

"Never, in the field of human conflict, was so much owed by so many to so few," Churchill said of the RAF pilots during the Battle of Britain. Here some of "The Few" rest while they can.

so serious the British had no other choice but to take it on the chin in the Atlantic and wait for the invasion force to steam across the Channel. Without a doubt, this was the darkest hour of the Allied cause.

That summer, Doenitz's crews took the lessons of 1939 to heart and changed tactics. In the first months of the war, the subs either operated as lone wolves or attempted to attack in packs with a tactical commander on scene to direct the operations. Pack tactics only worked against convoys, but the 1939 skirmishes in the Atlantic rarely saw the undersea boats even encounter these targets. Of all the ships lost before summer of 1940, only about a half dozen had been sunk in convoys.

From the air, a standard forty-ship convoy seemed to stretch to the horizon. In reality, it occupied only a few square miles of ocean. As Allied shipping was concentrated into these convoys, the Atlantic grew barren of targets for the U-boats. No longer could the U-boats sit astride the sea lanes to pick off stragglers or ships sailing independently. The rest were stragglers or vessels steaming alone. As such targets grew scarce, the U-boats had to hit the convoys. Finding them was the challenge.

Admiral Raeder and Luftwaffe chief Herman Goering did not get along. Their animosity damaged chances of close air-sea cooperation in the North Atlantic exactly at a time when Doenitz needed long-range air reconnaissance to detect Allied convoys. Without such an asset, he was forced to rely on sightings by his own U-boats or signals intelligence as developed by the Kriegsmarine's code breakers, known as B-Dienst.

Above: The Battle of Britain raged through the summer of 1940. Here, fire crews extinguish a blaze after a German air raid on London. *Below:* If the Germans had been able to seize France's modern warships, the balance of power in the Mediterranean could have shifted decisively against the Royal Navy. Even worse, those fleet elements, in German hands, could have been used to support an invasion of the Home Islands themselves.

Prime Minister Winston Churchill was so concerned about France's armistice with Germany in 1940 that he ordered his fleet to destroy the French fleet in North Africa if it refused to surrender or join the British. Tragically, more than a thousand French sailors were killed by British shellfire.

Submarines made poor scouting platforms. Their low silhouette limited their field of view to a few miles a best. The U-boats also lacked surface radar, which meant Doenitz's command had to rely on optics and eyeballs.

In the summer of 1940, B-Dienst supplied excellent information on the Allied convoy in the North Atlantic. Doenitz used that intelligence to personally direct wolf packs from shore, abandoning the concept of having a tactical commander on scene. With one boat shadowing the detected convoy and reporting any changes in speed or course, Doenitz would concentrate his available boats on the Allies to try to overwhelm the escort force.

To pull off such interceptions took luck, skill, and timing. The subs could not operate too far east toward Ireland and England, as they ran the risk of encountering Coastal Command's aircraft. At the same time, their

limited range prevented interception too far west into the central North Atlantic. Thus, in 1940, there was a sweet spot in the convoy lanes where, if the Germans were lucky enough to find a convoy, their U-boats could shadow and attack for several days. Hitting that mark became almost an art form.

That September, the wolf pack attacks began in earnest. Doenitz had the intelligence he needed from B-Dienst; he had the boats on line out in the North Atlantic, and his U-boats were crewed by seasoned men led by aggressive and innovative skippers. The confluence of all these things came together in a series of clashes that marked a new phase in the war at sea.

On August, 28, 1940, B-Dienst decoded a British radio message to convoy SC-2, which was set to depart from Sydney, Nova Scotia, at the beginning of September.

Much of the French fleet remained at Toulon, out of the Royal Navy's reach. Throughout the war, the Allies launched air attacks on these vessels. In 1942, after the Allied invasion of North Africa, the French fleet scuttled itself rather than fall into German hands, though the air attacks on Toulon continued. By the time Toulon was finally liberated in 1944, there was almost nothing left of France's naval power.

THE NAZI CODE BREAKERS

After the revelation of the Ultra secret in the 1970s, historians have focused on the Allied code-breaking successes during World War II. Less well known are the achievements of the Third Reich's cryptologists. Before the war, the Germans built a chain of radio intercept stations along the coast in order to detect French, English, and American transmissions. The German navy's signals intelligence branch, known as B-Dienst, exploited the data gathered by these stations. This code-breaking effort, spearheaded by the brilliant Wilhelm Tranow, yielded incredible results, unrivaled by any other German intel service. B-Dienst analysts penetrated various British, French, Dutch, American, and Russian naval codes. In the early years of the war, B-Dienst was reading much of the Royal Navy's mail, having broken British Naval Cipher No. 3 and the merchant shipping code. They were also able to read, at least for a short time, at least one high-level Royal Navy command cipher.

These successes gave Adm. Karl Doenitz the location and routes used by the Allied convoys crossing the North Atlantic. He exploited that information and based his own patrol lines on B-Dienst's intel. Later, Doenitz credited his navy code breakers with providing more than half the actionable intelligence developed during the U-boat campaign. With the Luftwaffe providing minimal support at best through most of the war, B-Dienst became one of the few means to find convoys in the Atlantic beyond the eyeballs of Doenitz's U-boat crews.

After 1943, the signals intelligence dried up. The British changed their codes and the B-Dienst's offices in Berlin were bombed to rubble. Much of the information the code breakers had painstakingly collected over the years did not survive the air raids. B-Dienst moved to a small village outside of Berlin to carry on operations until the advancing Russians forced the service to relocate one final time to Flensburg.

Even seventy years later, little has been written on this vital naval intelligence branch, and its effect on the naval war still is not fully understood.

The signal detailed the convoy's mid-ocean rendezvous point with the escort force that would shepherd it to English ports. This priceless bit of intel gave Doenitz time to lay an ambush with four of his boats.

Composed of fifty-three merchant ships, SC-2 was a slow convoy whose vessels carried lumber, wheat, sugar, iron ore, steel for England's factories, oil, and phosphate. The effort to sustain Britain was a multinational task. Ships in SC-3 belonged to Greece, Holland, Norway, and Denmark.

On September 6, Kapitänleutnant Hans Gerit von Stockhausen's *U-65* found the convoy right where B-Dienst had predicted. He radioed a contact report and shadowed the Allied ships. The convoy's escorts spotted his boat on the surface and attacked him. Though only thirty-two, Von Stockhausen was a veteran submariner on his fourth war patrol of the year. Seeing the British escorts closing on his boat, he ordered his boat deep. After a cursory hunt for him, the escort sped back to the convoy. Von Stockhausen surfaced and looped ahead of SC-2.

During the pursuit, a force eight gale blew through this stretch of the North Atlantic, generating heaving seas and fierce winds. Battling through the weather, *U-65* regained contact and directed the three other boats onto the convoy.

Gunther Prien intercepted SC-2 on the night of September 7, 1940. Around 0330, he waded into the convoy on the surface. His first target was the W. A. Souter & Company steamship *Neptunian*, which carried 8,500 tons of sugar from Santiago, Chile. Prien's first two torpedoes missed. His third slammed into the

Above: With much of Britain's destroyers tied down in England awaiting the expected Nazi invasion, the onus of protecting the sea lanes fell on smaller, less capable escorts that posed little threat to U-boats. *Below:* A U-boat crew in formation on their submarine's forward deck. With only a handful of subs, Doenitz's force ran riot in the Atlantic, sinking so many Allied merchant ships that his crews called the second half of 1940 "The Happy Time."

Neptunian, and the five thousand–ton vessel capsized and sank in seven minutes. The entire crew of thirty-six died in the attack.

An hour later, Prien struck again. This time, he targeted the *Jose de Larringa*, a British steamer heavily laden with 5,300 tons of steel and linseed oil. While his forward torpedo room crew reloaded their tubes, Prien fired a stern shot that broke the *Jose de Larringa*'s back. The vessel split in two and sank eleven minutes later. Her crew of forty died to the last man.

Prien's veterans finished reloading the forward tubes, and he maneuvered for a third attack. At 0533, he singled out the Norwegian freighter *Gro*, which had escaped from the Nazi invasion of her home country to reach England in the spring of 1940. Carrying six thousand tons of wheat, she was typical of the vessels that kept the British population fed during the summer of 1940.

Prien put a fish in her starboard side. The hit ruptured her boilers, sending gouts of steam into the air. The engine room crew burned to death as the ship broke in half. In the vessel's final seconds, two men jumped

Above: A U-boat at sea. Without radar in 1940, the subs were hard-pressed to find convoys in the Atlantic's vast expanse, making the code breakers of B-Dienst vital to the campaign. *Below left:* Two U-boat sailors occupy some of their down time by chatting and building a model of their submarine. *Below right:* "Silent Otto" Kretschmer was one of the great U-boat aces of World War II. In his two years in the Atlantic, he and his crew sank forty-seven Allied ships, totaling 274,333 tons.

Through the first year of the war, U-boats feasted on ships sailing independently. Only a handful were sunk while in convoys. That changed in the fall of 1940.

from the bridge and climbed into a small life raft. Their lifeless bodies were found twenty days later by the *Flower*-class corvette, HMS *Periwinkle.* The rest of the crew escaped in a lifeboat, spending over three days in the storm before being rescued.

At dawn, Prien broke off his attack to shadow the convoy just as *U-28* reached the area. On the night of September 9, 1940, both boats waded into SC-2 again. *U-28* was commanded by Guenter Kuhnke, a superb skipper who received one of the submarine force's first Iron Cross awards for actions in September 1939. A year later, he had eleven ships to his credit and was on his fifth war patrol. He and Prien made a formidable team.

The Bull of Scapa Flow made the first attack that night. He evaded the screen and got in among the merchant ships. His first spread missed the intended target, but one of the torpedoes streaked into the neighboring column of vessels and blew the Greek steamer *Possidon* out of the water. Seventeen men and five thousand tons of phosphate went down with her.

Prien pushed his luck that night. After completing this attack, another merchant ship bore down on him in the darkness. He evaded it, but came within fifty meters of a collision. Somehow, with all the chaos, the weather, and the lack of illumination, the Allied ship failed to sight *U-47.*

Four hours later, Kuhnke destroyed his twelfth ship. He targeted the *Mardinian*, hitting her under the bridge. She went down with six of her crew with her cargo load of 3,500 tons of pitch.

Dawn broke and the U-boats reverted to stalking mode again. These night surface attacks caught the British escorts totally by surprise. With surface search radars yet to be installed on most of the antisubmarine warfare fleet, the Royal Navy ships had no way of detecting this method of attack short of the Mark One eyeball. The U-boat's low silhouette in heavy seas made spotting them at night virtually impossible. The boats could slip in and out of the convoy without fear of being picked up by British ASDIC (sonar) systems, since those only detected objects under water.

A moment in "The Happy Time."

The Germans had found a chink in the convoy armor. In the weeks ahead, they would exploit it with ruthless efficiency.

Convoy SC-2 reached England after losing nearly 10 percent of its ships. The disaster served as a wakeup call to the British. Their convoys—escorted or not—had been steaming virtually without interference since the war began. That luxury was over.

A week later, convoy SC-3 ran into Kapitänleutnant Heinrich Bleichrodt. In a series of running, lone wolf attacks, his boat, *U-48*, sank six ships. While stalking SC-3, he ran into an outbound convoy and sank two merchant vessels from it as well.

As Bleichrodt picked off his targets, *U-47* took up weather reporting duty for the Luftwaffe. Prien had expended all but one of his torpedoes, so Doenitz tasked him with this mind-numbing duty. Twice

a day, he radioed in the current conditions so Goering's commanders could plan and prepare their attacks on England.

On September 20, convoy HX-72 sailed right over Prien. Abandoning his meteorological mission, the cagey Nazi commander shadowed the convoy as Doenitz marshaled his forces. HX-72 consisted of forty-two ships arrayed in nine columns, covered at first by two Canadian destroyers and the auxiliary cruiser *Jervis Bay*. At this point in the war, the escorts from Canada could not cover their chargees all the way to the rendezvous point with the escort coming from the Royal Navy's Western Approaches Command. This mid-ocean gap left the convoys hopelessly vulnerable if detected. In HX-72's case, that gap would last for just over twenty hours before the Home Isles–based escorts reached it four hundred miles west of Ireland.

The weather had been brutal during this crossing. On the eighteenth, three days before Prien encountered HX-72, the convoy was hit by a northwest gale. Titanic waves crashed over bows, hammering bridges with green water, smashing lifeboats to matchsticks, and throwing cargo around in holds. Exhausted, the merchant seamen worked to keep their heavily loaded ships afloat through the storm. Three days later, they faced the horror of the war's second major wolf pack attack, conducted by the best U-boat skippers of World War II.

For twenty-four hours, five subs savaged the convoy. Besides Bleichrodt and Prien, Doenitz sent in Otto Kretschmer (*U-99*), Joachim Schepke (*U-100*)—who would sink more ships than any other submariner before his death—and Hans Jenich (*U-32*). Jenich would sink seventeen ships and damage three more before he was captured in October 1940.

The conditions were perfect for the submariners: Full moon and flat seas in the wake of that violent storm. Hunting by moonlight, Kretschmer struck the first blow. Nicknamed "Silent Otto," Kretschmer possessed a razor-sharp mind with the panache of a romantic. Before the war, he studied English literature at Exeter University. Now, at age twenty-eight, Kretschmer's mastery of U-boat warfare had catapulted him into the national spotlight back in Germany. He'd sunk twenty-two ships and was now on his fourteenth war patrol. He'd been one of the first U-boat commanders to pioneer close-range night surface attack tactics. Now he unleashed them on HX-72.

Shortly after 0300 on September 21, after slipping past the escort screen, Silent Otto torpedoed the British tanker *Invershannon*. Down by the bow, with fifteen dead, the crew abandoned ship.

U-boat victims. Merchant sailors are hauled aboard a passing Allied ship. These men were the lucky ones. Others drifted at sea for weeks, sometimes months, as they watched their shipmates slowly die of exposure.

An hour later, Kretschmer set up his second attack. Closing to five meters, his crew put a fish into the 3,600-ton steamer *Baron Blythswood*. With her holds filled with iron ore, she sank in forty seconds. There were no survivors.

Thirty minutes later, *U-99* struck again, this time crippling the Glasgow-based *Elmbank* with a hit on her starboard side from a thousand meters away. She fell out of the convoy and was set upon by both Prien and Kretschmer, who tried to finish her off with their deck guns. After firing almost a hundred shells, they succeeded in setting her afire, but she refused to go down. Kretschmer used his last two torpedoes to polish off the *Elmbank* and *Invershannon*.

Before heading for home, Kretschmer doubled back along HX-72's track. Earlier on his patrol, he had spotted a lone seaman bobbing on the waves in a tiny raft. Miraculously, he found the man again after a short search. He brought him aboard, warmed him with

brandy and blankets, then took him back to the scene of the previous night's destruction until he located a British lifeboat. He guided *U-99* alongside; passed out blankets, food, and water; and transferred his prisoner to the lifeboat. Before departing, he gave the Allied sailors a compass heading for Ireland.

Schepke, Bleichrodt, and Jenich added to Kretschmer's carnage, sinking another ten ships. HX-72 limped into England with a quarter of its vessels lost, its surviving seamen tested to the utmost of their endurance by their voyage.

Of the forty-two ships in HX-72, thirty-one were destroyed during the war. Thirteen went down during the September 20 to 21 battle alone, another eighteen ended up on the Atlantic's lightless bottom as the war progressed. The grinding battle of attrition in the harsh North Atlantic not only determined England's future survival, but it also destroyed a generation's worth of merchant shipping as well.

Above: The pathetic state of the Royal Navy's Fleet Air Arm required help from the United States to solve. The Grumman Wildcat, called Martlet by the FAA, became the Royal Navy's first modern carrier-based fighter. Here, British officers pose in front of a freshly acquired Grumman. *Right:* A U-boat crew celebrates a successful patrol. *Opposite:* An Allied convoy sails through an Atlantic dusk. In a few hours, the boats would surface and prey upon these mostly unarmed vessels.

CHAPTER FIVE

LONG KNIVES

The sharks sortied from Lorient in early October. First out were Kapitänleutnant Fritz Frauenheim's *U-101*, Johann Mohr's *U-124*, and Bleichrodt's *U-48*, all three slipping from the docks and steaming west for the North Atlantic hunting grounds on October 5. Schepke departed on October 12, followed by Kretschmer the next day and Prien the day after. By October 15, 1940, the most deadly U-boat captains of the war were concentrating on the convoy lanes near the Rockall Bank.

The British were not prepared.

After a year of war, the convoy system still did not have 100 percent buy in from the stubborn and independent-minded merchant skippers. As more of Britain's prewar fleet hit the bottom, the flow of food and supplies to England relied increasingly on Allied and neutral shipping—the Norwegians, Dutch, Swedes, and Greeks. They tolerated the confines and the constraints of the convoys with impatience and frustration. The Greeks especially had a habit of either straggling behind the convoys or romping ahead of them.

The U-boats gladly picked them off. Alone, undefended, hardly ever bothering to zig-zag or change course, these merchant skippers lived in a state of self-centered denial that often cost them their ships, their crews, and their own lives. Against the likes of Kretschmer and Prien, they stood no chance, especially at time when even well-defended convoys were savaged by these cunning and aggressive captains.

Convoy SC-7 left Canada on October 5, the same day *U-101* and *U-48* set out from Lorient. Composed of thirty-five ships and eventually seven escorts, SC-7 carried vital war material. The SS *Beatus* and *Fiscus* were full of aircraft destined for the RAF; another steamer held hundreds of trucks desperately needed by the post-Dunkirk Royal Army. Others carried steel ingots forged in mills in Sydney, Canada; timber and pulpwood from the forests of British Columbia; iron ore to keep the factories functioning in the Home Isles; and grain to feed those who labored in them.

Things went wrong from the outset. A day of out Canada, one steamer suffered mechanical failure and aborted the voyage. Down to thirty-four ships, it did not take long for the more obstinate skippers to make life difficult for the convoy commodore, Vice Adm. Lachlan Donald Ian Mackinnon. Some of the ships struggled to

(continued on page 92)

Opposite: An Allied convoy prepares to depart. Until late 1941, American merchant ships were officially forbidden to travel into the European war zone.

THE ITALIANS IN THE ATLANTIC

In June 1940, the Italian navy joined the Atlantic convoy war when three boats were sent to patrol off the Azores. The Regia Marina deployed twenty-eight submarines to Bordeaux later in 1940. Known to the Italians as Bordeaux Sommergibile, or BETASOM, the concrete sub pens the Germans constructed there became the center of Italian operations in the Atlantic. Adm. Karl Doenitz assigned them secondary areas of operation outside the main convoy lanes in the North Atlantic.

The Italians scored some successes, but showed they did not have the killer instinct Doenitz expected of his crews. On August 12, 1940, the Italian submarine *Malaspina* intercepted convoy OB-193 and made a surface attack on the eight thousand–ton tanker *British Fame*. When the boat's watch detected the convoy, the Italian skipper was reportedly dozing in a deckchair. The sub launched five torpedoes at the *British Fame* and had to dive once to avoid being hit by return gunfire. The tanker went

An Italian *Sirena*-class submarine. Twelve of these boats were completed in the mid-1930s, and only one survived the war. This boat, *Zaffiro*, met its end in the Mediterranean in June 1942. In all, thirty-three Italian subs operated in the Atlantic during World War II, where they sank 109 Allied ships totaling almost six hundred thousand tons.

Italian fleet subs on maneuvers. In 1941, the U-boat crews had total faith that they would soon strangle Britain and force England out of the war.

down eventually and earned distinction as the first Allied vessel sunk by an Italian submarine. In a gallant gesture, the *Malaspina*'s skipper took the *British Fame*'s lifeboats in tow for twenty-fours to bring the crew to a safe location.

The Axis conducted few joint operations in the Atlantic—a fact that stands in stark contrast to the way the Anglo-American alliance operated. By late 1940, the Italian boats were destroying about 200 tons of merchant shipping a day. The Germans averaged about 1,100.

Later in the war, seven of the Italian boats based at BETASOM were reconfigured to conduct long-range cargo missions to the Far East. Two of these boats were sunk in transit and three were captured by the Germans following Italy's surrender in September 1943.

The BETASOM submarine pens still stand today and are open to the public.

One of Doenitz's gray wolves heads out on patrol.

(continued from page 89)
keep station simply due their worn-out engines. The convoy designation SC stood for Slow Convoy, and these would steam usually at about eight knots. That proved too much for some, and they fell out of formation and dropped back behind the main convoy. Others were conned by skippers who either feared attack within the convoy or simply did not care to follow orders from the Royal Navy.

That was a rugged road to travel. On October 16, 1940, straggler SS *Trevisa*, a Canadian steamer loaded with timber products, crossed paths with *U-124*, which had been busy with weather reporting duty west of Rockall Bank. Her skipper, Johann Mohr, was on his second patrol and had two ships to his credit. He gave chase and sank *Trevisa* late that night. Seven of her crew died, while fourteen ended up in the rolling Atlantic swells.

On the night of October 16 and into the early hours of October 17, 1940, Convoy SC-7 was down to thirty ships in formation. Four more straggled behind the main force. Only two sloops and a corvette were left to screen the convoy. Aboard *U-48*, Bleichrodt's lookouts spotted SC-7 lumbering through the dark autumn night.

Kapitänleutnant "Ajax" Bleichrodt had been with the U-boat fleet since 1939. He'd taken over as skipper of *U-48* a month before. His aggressiveness had netted him eight ships and an Iron Cross. Now on his second patrol, he stalked SC-7 until dawn on the seventeenth.

Once in position, he struck fiercely. *U-48* loosed a three-torpedo spread at the convoy, each "eel" aimed at a different ship. At the time, Bleichrodt thought all three found their targets. In reality, one missed. The other two slammed into the 9,512-ton British tanker *Languedoc* and the SS *Scoresby*, a 3,800-ton merchant

Above: The Germans constructed enormous bomb-proof U-boat pens in several key French ports following France's surrender in June 1940. The Royal Navy repeatedly asked the RAF to bomb these construction sites to delay or derail their completion, but Bomber Command considered such attacks a diversion to their strategic bombing campaign and refused. *Below left:* Dawn in the North Atlantic. In 1940, the daylight hours usually brought a respite from U-boat attacks. *Below right:* Two boats preparing for sea. The fall of 1940 saw some of the most one-sided convoy actions of the war. The German U-boats attacked at night on the surface. Until the advent of reliable radar, these tactics were brutally effective.

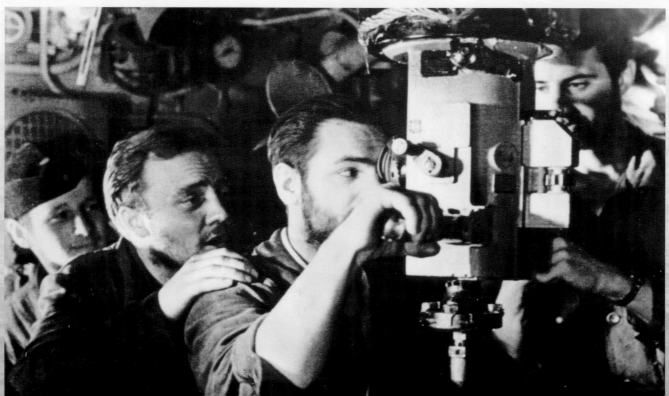

Above: While the convoys were ravaged by the likes of Prien and Kretschmer that fall, fast liners like the *Queen Elizabeth* (seen here) made swift transatlantic crossings, often alone. Their high top speed made them difficult targets for U-boats. *Opposite top:* Merchant mariners assigned to crew tankers had a particularly dangerous job. When hit, tankers often caught fire and spewed flaming oil across the surface, making escape impossible for their crews. Here a tanker burns in her death agony. *Opposite bottom:* A U-boat crew stalks its prey while at periscope depth. Most of the German boats were not true submarines, but rather submersibles capable of staying under water for only a short duration.

ship full of lumber designed for use as supports in coal mines.

Before *U-48* could attack again, a Sunderland flying boat swooped down on the boat as it ran on the surface. The sudden strike forced Bleichrodt to crash-dive, and he lost contact with the convoy for the rest of the day.

No matter. Doenitz had unleashed the hounds. Six more U-boats would soon join the battle.

Four hours after the *Languedoc* took a hit, Heinrich Liebe's boat, *U-38*, ran across the Greek steamer *Aenos*. The vessel was overloaded with 6,276 tons of wheat and was wallowing in the Atlantic swells when the Germans encountered her straggling behind SC-7. Liebe tracked her from periscope depth before launching a G7e torpedo just before 1000 on October 17. The torpedo crippled *Aenos* but failed to sink her. Liebe, showing the daring and aggressiveness that had already earned him a Knight's Cross, surfaced near the Greek vessel. Despite the threat of air attack, he sent his gun crew out on deck to shell the *Aenos* into submission. The 3,500-tonner sank an hour later.

The aces had drawn blood. Liebe and Bleichrodt were among the top surviving U-boat skippers of World War II. Liebe eventually went on to sink thirty-four

A tanker goes down, her back broken by a direct hit amidships.

ships for 187,267 tons, while Bleichrodt (who earned his Knight's Cross for his attacks in October 1940) destroyed sixteen ships in his first two patrols. He finished with twenty-four to his credit, totaling 157,260 tons.

For the next two days and nights, SC-7 steamed through a gauntlet of U-boat attacks. Though reinforced by an additional sloop and corvette, the escort force stood no chance against the German onslaught. All night long, ships exploded and burned. Men died trapped within the steel hulls of their sinking ships. Others met their end after leaping overboard and into the frigid Atlantic. By dawn on the eighteenth, the course of SC-7's crucible could be traced for miles by the debris, desperate survivors, and oil slicks left behind by the sixteen ships that the U-boats had destroyed.

Altogether, *U-101*, *U-46*, *U-99*, *U-123*, *U-100*, and *U-38* scored kills. Otto Kretschmer in *U-99* set the standard for the bloodletting. Late on the night of October 18, he charged into the convoy, nearly getting rammed while he maneuvered wildly on the surface. Firing from point-blank range—seven hundred yards in one case—Kretschmer's furious assault sank the SS *Empire Miniver*, SS *Niritos,* and the SS *Fiscus*. In that one attack, *U-99* sent to the bottom 5,426 tons of sulphur, several squadrons worth of crated aircraft, and enough steel to make an entire armored division's worth of Matilda II heavy tanks.

After midnight on the nineteenth, Kretschmer unleashed all his torpedoes. His aim was true: three more ships went down, giving him a total of six on the night.

Above: Rearming a U-boat fresh from patrol in one of the French port submarine pens. Without those enormous concrete structures, operations from France would have been almost impossible, as the threat from air attack would have been too great by 1941. *Below:* A U-boat crew plotting its next attack.

Italian submarines under attack in the Atlantic. In the fall of 1940, Italy sent a significant submarine force into the Atlantic. Doenitz found these subs to be generally ineffective.

Merchant seamen, survivors of a sinking, line up for chow after being rescued.

They included the SS *Empire Brigade*, SS *Thalia*, and SS *Snefjeld*. The *Thalia*, a 5,800-ton Greek steamer heavily laden with a cargo of steel, lead, and zinc, sank in under a minute after taking a torpedo hit in the bow. Only four of her crew survived.

Kapitänleutnant Engelbert Endrass also scored high that night. Commanding *U-46*, Endrass was a highly respected ace who had earned his Knight's Cross for sinking a dozen ships in his first three patrols during the summer of 1940. Prior to taking his own boat out, he had served under Prien in *U-47* and had taken part in the Scapa Flow raid.

Endrass attacked convoy SC-7 around 2000 on October 18, scoring two hits with four torpedoes. Two hours later, he sank the Swedish steamer SS *Gunborg*, giving him three ships and more than eight thousand tons on the night. This included the 4,885-ton *Beatus*, which was loaded with steel, lumber, and American aircraft.

When dawn mercifully broke on the morning of the nineteenth, the U-boats melted away. Altogether, SC-7 lost twenty of its ships. Another six had been damaged. Over the next two days, the survivors limped into British ports while the corvette HMS *Bluebell* scoured the waves for survivors.

Winter in the Atlantic. The convoys still made the passage to England, but heavy swells and storm-tossed seas hammered their escorts. In such conditions, ASDIC was almost useless, and visibility was so bad it was difficult to detect a surfaced submarine even in daylight.

But the slaughter did not end with SC-7's near destruction. Sailing directly behind SC-7 was HX-79, a lightly escorted convoy of forty-nine merchantmen. As the SC-7 was torn apart by Doenitz's wolves, the British admiralty sped reinforcements to HX-79, fearing it would suffer a similar fate. Four corvettes, three auxiliaries, and two fast destroyers rendezvoused with the convoy just as it reached the Western Approaches.

Gunther Prien spotted HX-79 on October 19, 1940. Doenitz ordered all available U-boats to strike the convoy. Three of the subs that had destroyed SC-7 had empty tubes, so they headed for home. That left four boats plus Prien's to make the attack.

On the night of the nineteenth, Prien surfaced and crept past the British screen on the south side of the convoy. Endrass did the same on the north side. What followed was another holocaust of flaming, exploding ships. With the Germans moving within the convoy while surfaced, the British escorts could not detect them with their ASDIC sensors. As ship after ship went down, the escorts threw out star shells and sped back and forth along the convoy's flanks, searching in vain for targets.

Not a German sub was hit. The aces feasted on HX-79 all night long. Endrass sank two, as did Liebe. Schepke took out three more, and Bleichrodt destroyed the 6,000-ton British taker *Shirak*.

Prien was the master once again. He struck six ships, four of which went to the bottom. A fifth was polished off by *U-48*. Altogether, *U-47* removed more than 20,000 tons of shipping from the Allied cause. Fully loaded, these four ships carried 10,000 tons of steel, 9,400 tons of lumber, 1,700 tons of lead and zinc, and

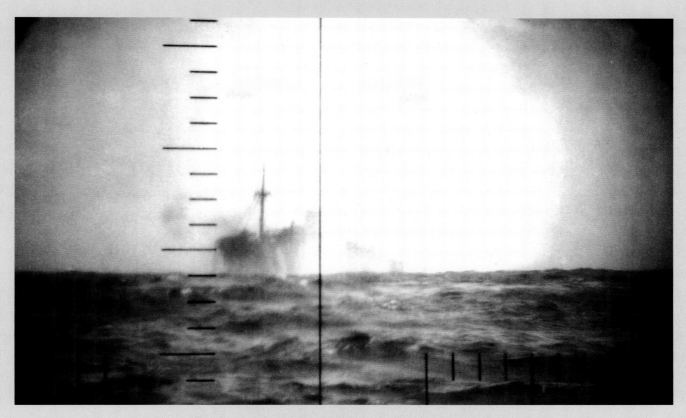

Above: A comparatively rare submerged daylight attack. Such tactics became more common later in the war as Allied escorts were better equipped with radar and the mid-Atlantic air gap was narrowed. *Below left:* An Allied airman's view of a surfaced U-boat. Their narrow hulls, short length, and low profile made them difficult to spot, especially in rough weather. *Below right:* On the surface in daylight and in foul weather, a U-boat's crew watches one of its victims succumb to a torpedo attack.

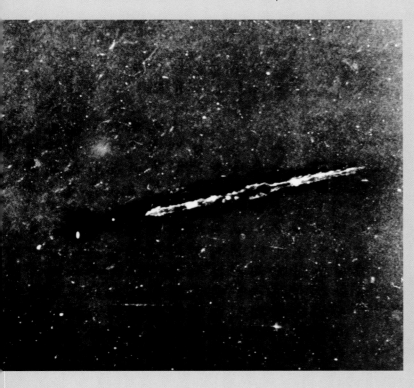

Above left: A survivor, cast adrift for days after his ship went down, is discovered by an Allied patrol vessel. In the North Atlantic, men who were unable to get into a raft or lifeboat rarely survived for long in the water. *Above right:* Merchant mariners were highly capable and enterprising men. When their ships went down, they improvised with whatever they had to help ensure their survival. Here, a lifeboat has been rigged with sails and is making for dry land. *Below:* A U-boat's triumphant return.

A wall of water about to sweep over the bow of a merchantman somewhere in the Atlantic. Often, the ravages of mother nature did more damage that German U-boats.

8,300 tons of sugar. At a time when every pound of war material was desperately needed, this one night's work on the part of Germany's premier submarine crew was simply devastating.

The aces sank twelve of HX-79's forty-nine ships. In one furious engagement, the Allies lost 75,000 tons of shipping to Germany's greatest U-boat commanders.

The destruction of SC-7 and the casualties inflicted on HX-79 represent the highest losses suffered in a two-day period by the Allies during the war. The Germans who fought these twin engagements memorialized them as the Nights of Long Knives.

November and December were no better for the British. German and Italian submarines swept the seas, inflicting devastating losses whenever they encountered a convoy. The U-boats sank another sixty-nine ships in November and December despite the worsening weather.

On December 1, 1940, seven U-boats and three Italian subs caught HX-90 en route to the British Isles and sank ten merchantmen. The damage dealt to HX-90 was typical of the success the Axis had that fall. Between September 2 and December 2, 1940, the wolf packs sank 150 seven ships, totaling 847,000 tons. Three U-boats were lost.

The attacks began to have a strategic impact. Oil imports to Britain plunged 50 percent by year's end. What was getting through the wolf packs covered only two-thirds of the Empire's consumption. The British were forced to subsist off their reserves to make up the difference, a desperate measure that could not be sustained for long, as Japan found out in 1943 and 1944. The British had to turn things around, or their country's war effort would be throttled on the Western Approaches.

Winston Churchill recognized the crisis all too well. Toward the end of 1940, he wrote a letter to President Roosevelt and flatly told him that Britain's future lay on the seas in 1941.

CHAPTER SIX

LIFE IN THE BOATS

For both sides, the Atlantic war was fought with degrees of human misery rarely seen in other theaters of war. Not only did the men face horrifying deaths to fire, drowning, and underwater pressure, but they also endured some of the worst weather on the planet. From freezing temperatures so cold that ice would form on the faces of those who stood watch, to 140-degree heat in the engine rooms during cruises to the tropics, the U-boat men endured polar extremes through the years. And with their Spartan submarines devoid of creature comforts, there was no respite from the constant physical toll the conditions inflicted. Within days of being at sea, the boats reeked with a mix of body odor, human feces, diesel oil, and filth. While submerged, the men used buckets set out between their boat's engines as toilets. Depth charging or radical maneuvers meant the buckets spilled over, leaving the engineering crewmembers to work among excrement.

The men hot bunked—shared beds—because there wasn't enough room to give each submariner his own space. They lived atop the food they would eat—crates of supplies, fresh fruit, and vegetables were crammed into every possible space before departing on a patrol. Yet often at the tail end of long operations, the men were reduced to eating the dregs of their provisions, as the boats simply did not have the space to keep the crews well fed for extended periods of time.

Doenitz, who had experienced all the hardships of life in the boats during World War I, recognized the importance of giving his men all the luxuries and comforts available in wartime Europe once they returned home from patrol. Special recreational areas were established for them, and cheap liquor was made readily available. The partying that took place—portrayed in the classic film, *Das Boot*—served as a pressure valve that helped drain away the incredible levels of stress and tension the men were under every time they set sail for the Atlantic. But even with the hotels, the special leave trains to Germany, the booze, and the comfort of French women, the psychological trauma each patrol inflicted was cumulative. A man could only take so much, and at times in the midst of terrifying depth-charge attacks, or surface battles, breakdowns occurred. A few, even officers, committed suicide.

The photos in these following pages give insight into the experience of the average German U-boat sailor.

Opposite: Erich Topp survived the war as the third-ranking U-boat ace of the Atlantic campaign. He sank *Reuben James* in October 1941. During Operation Drumroll, Topp attacked SS *David Atwater* off Cape Charles, Virginia. As the crew tried to abandon ship, Topp's men continued to fire their deck guns, killing all but three of the *Atwater*'s crew. Coast guard vessels found drifting lifeboats riddled with bullet holes and filled with the dead.

Above left: In the claustrophobic confines of a Type VII's forward torpedo room. The men there languished in wet, humid, and frequently broiling hot conditions. Fierce storms also contributed to their physical misery. *Above right:* Looking scruffy after weeks on patrol, a U-boat crew shares a rare moment of levity. When forced to live for weeks at a time practically on top of each other in an environment devoid of privacy or personal space, the crews either grew incredibly close or fractured over personality and leadership issues. *Below left:* Standing watch while on the surface meant long hours, scanning the horizon for potential targets or potential threats. One lapse could cost the lives of every man aboard his boat. *Below right:* A U.S. Navy escort depth charges a submerged U-boat. Few things were more terrifying to a submariner than such an attack. The men could hear the splashes of the depth charges as they entered the water. The blasts would shatter gauges, knock fillings loose, and wreak havoc on their boat's electrical systems. These attacks sometimes went on for hours as escorts dropped dozens of charges. Some of the men cracked under the strain.

Above: After weeks of boredom, stark moments of terror, and shared misery, a torpedo room crew celebrates the ultimate payoff: scoring kills during a convoy attack.

Left: Swimming in the Baltic during an operational work-up. Crews bonded during those long training cycles, and even as the war grew more intense and losses mounted, Doenitz resisted cutting short that work-up period.

Above left: Commander Braeutigam, a prewar skipper, poses during maneuvers in 1935. Most of the prewar U-boat officers were either killed in action during 1939 to 1943, or they survived by being promoted out of their boats to flotilla command or above. *Above right:* Some of the forty-four men from *U-664* who survived their boat's sinking by USS *Card*'s air group. They're seen here after being rescued by a U.S. Navy destroyer. *Below:* *U-2322* off the coast of Northern Ireland in April 1945. A Type XXIII boat, she was the only one of her class to carry out two war patrols before V-E Day. Her crew sank a solitary British cargo ship before the surrender.

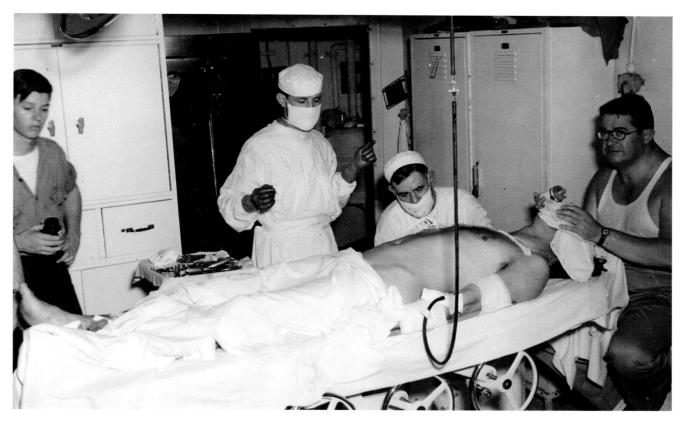

Above: A medical team operates on one of *U-664*'s survivors. He'd been hit by a .50-caliber machine gun bullet in the arm while abandoning ship. Such a fate was a lucky one: a U-boat crewman had about a 25 percent chance to survive the war. *Below:* Exhausted U-boat crewmen aboard USS *Core* in August 1943. On the twenty-fourth of that month, the *Core*'s air group sank both *U-84* and *U-185* in a series of spectacularly successful attacks.

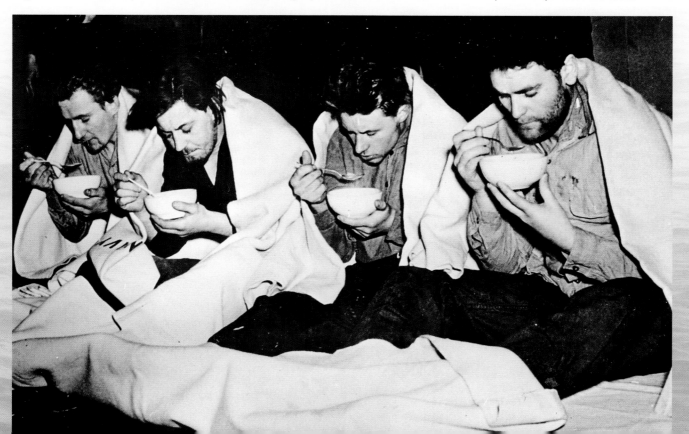

Above left: U-boat crewman read and reread letters from home until they were tattered and worn. Such notes from loved ones became lifelines for these young men. *Above right:* A U-boat takes a hit during a surprise airstrike. By 1943, the weapons used by Allied patrol aircraft had been significantly upgraded and included such technological marvels as the FIDO homing torpedo. *Below:* Aircraft from the USS *Core* attack *U-84* on August 23, 1943. The boat survived this onslaught, only to be tracked down and sunk the following day.

Above: At the end of the war, the surviving boats surfaced and surrendered to the nearest Allied vessels. On May 22, some of those boats, now prizes of war, were sailed up the Thames to be displayed at trophies at Westminster. This photograph captures their triumphant arrival. *Below left:* The end of a U-boat off Gibraltar in February 1944. Here, two U.S. Navy PBY Catalinas from VP-63 joined forces with a pair of British destroyers to ensure this boat would share the fate of 782 of her sister U-boats. *Below right:* Atlantic patrols made old men out of youthful submarine commanders. A few broke down under the strain, including one of *U-505*'s skippers who committed suicide during a depth-charge attack.

CHAPTER SEVEN

NIGHT OF THE ACES

After the bloodletting of 1940, the U-boat crews sensed victory was at hand. To them, it looked like the British were on the ropes. Imports were dropping, and the Home Isles were subsisting on a strict rationing. The British army was still disorganized and ill-equipped, and the Royal Navy had been stretched thin everywhere as its losses mounted and commitments grew. Construction of new warships and merchantmen were hampered by material shortages, available yard space, labor unrest, and the lack of modern facilities. Damaged ships made this situation worse—they clogged up the yards and slowed new construction.

The British were never closer to defeat than the end of 1940, even after winning the Battle of Britain. Another year like that and England would not be able to sustain her population, let alone keep the war effort going. The island nation's industry would grind to a halt as the flow of raw materials across the Atlantic was choked off. The citizens of England would face starvation. Churchill would have no choice but to make peace. If the Royal Navy could not keep the supply lines open across the seas, there was no hope of survival.

Admiral Karl Doenitz recognized that a pivotal moment in the war had arrived as well. He prepared his U-boat force to deliver the body blows that would bring Great Britain to its knees. Doenitz had cause for optimism. The small number of boats he had in the fight wreaking havoc on convoys would soon be heavily reinforced as the wartime construction program reached high gear. Doenitz's command was expanding so quickly that by mid-spring, he expected to have eighty brand-new boats working up in the Baltic Sea. Throwing that force into the fray certainly would tip the balance.

The key to a German victory in the Atlantic remained locating the Allied convoys. B-Dienst intercepts had played an important role in the successes of 1940, but the nature of the code war was such that Doenitz had to expect periods where B-Dienst would be unable to crack the latest British cipher changes. He had relied on his patrol lines to find the convoys, but what he really needed was air power cooperating with his command. In early 1941, Hitler ordered Reichmarshal Herman Goering to give Kampfgeschwader KG-40 to the Kriegsmarine. With KG-40's small force of four-engine Focke-Wulf Fw-200 Kondors under its operational control, the German navy now possessed an aerial reconnaissance force that could reach deep into the Atlantic. Based

Opposite: The convoys of 1941 were better protected than those ravaged by the U-boats in the fall of 1940. As the German spring offensive unfolded, the U-boat aces suddenly found convoys a far more dangerous nut to crack than they had during the previous fall.

Above: Hitler at an awards ceremony for some of Doenitz's wolves. After the fall of 1940, the undersea navy was riding high on a wave of successes and media attention. For the U-boat crews, 1941 started with total faith that they would soon strangle Britain and force her out of the war. *Below:* Wolfgang Lueth and his wife in Germany. Lueth sank forty-six merchant ships and a submarine in the course of his combat career. He commanded a variety of boats, including a Type IIB (*U-9*), a Type IXB long-range boat (*U-43*), and a Type IXD-2 (*U-181*). He was accidentally killed by a sentry in 1945. He was given the Third Reich's last state funeral before the war ended.

in Southwest France, the Kondors also proved to be a formidable antishipping platform.

There were other reasons for optimism in Lorient as New Year's Day 1941 arrived. During the fall of 1940, the U-boats validated Doenitz's coordinated wolf pack tactics. By attacking convoys on the surface at night, the Germans confounded British escorts as they struck with near impunity. The U-boat loss rate plunged even as their tonnage haul skyrocketed.

Doenitz wanted to build on that success with larger wolf packs and larger patrol lines that would integrate

Gunter Prien returns from another successful foray into the Atlantic. His death came as a big blow to the U-boat force.

their attacks with air and surface units. Such a triple threat would certainly overwhelm the Allied convoys and lead to even greater losses.

Doenitz spent January putting the pieces in play, starting with the Focke-Wulf Fw-200s. On January 7, 1941, KG-40 officially fell under the Kriegsmarine's operational control. The next day, the unit sank its first ship of the new campaign. Through January, KG-40 and the U-boat arm began working in close cooperation. Several times, Kondors detected convoys and directed U-boats onto them. On other occasions, the reverse happened. These early attempts met with mixed success as the kinks were sorted out. Frequently, the U-boats would go after a contact developed by KG-40, only to arrive too late to make an effective attack on the convoy. The same was sometimes true when the Kondors reacted to a U-boat contact.

Despite the coordination issues, the Kondors demonstrated their value in the tonnage war. During their first month under Doenitz's control, KG-40's crews sank fifteen ships totaling 57,770 tons. U-boats working contacts with the Kondors sank another seventeen. With time, the close coordination could pay off big dividends.

While aircrews and the submariners learned to work together, the Kriegsmarine launched Operation Berlin, a raiding mission commanded by Adm. Gunther Luetjens. Consisting of *Scharnhorst* and *Gneisenau*, Luetjens's task force had orders to pull the lion's tail with lightning fast hit-and-run raids against minimally defended North Atlantic convoys. If they encountered British capital ships, the Germans were to turn away and run.

Luetjens left Kiel on January 22, 1941. The British Home Fleet sailed from Scapa Flow in pursuit four days later. With two battleships, one battle cruiser,

By early 1941, the U-boat construction program yielded results, and Doenitz undertook a full-scale expansion of his undersea fleet.

eight cruisers, and eleven destroyers chasing his ships, Luetjens played a cagey cat-and-mouse game and repeatedly gave the Royal Navy the slip. *Scharnhorst* and *Gneisenau* both broke into the North Atlantic via the Denmark Straits, where for two months they ran the British ragged. When combined with the depredations of *Admiral Scheer* and *Admiral Hipper*, then tearing up the shipping lanes in the South Atlantic, plus the U-boats and Kondors, the British faced the most complex series of threats to their merchant trade during World War II.

It got ugly for the Brits. On February 8, 1941, *U-37* stumbled upon northbound convoy HG-53 southwest of Cape Vincent. Commanded by Kapitänleutnant Nicolai Clausen, *U-37* shadowed the convoy and relayed contact reports for KG-40. After dark, Clausen maneuvered into attack position and sank two ships before dawn. As the

sun rose and *U-37* fell back to shadow the convoy, the Kondors arrived to ensure the Allied seamen received no respite from attack. The Fw-200's dispatched five more ships. As the carnage unfolded, *Admiral Hipper* dashed for the scene. Convoy HG-53 faced a triple, air-sea-undersea threat without adequate defenses against any of them.

Clausen picked off another ship during a night attack in the early hours of February 10, and *Hipper* sank the straggling SS *Iceland*. The convoy limped into Britain after having lost nine ships. Had *Hipper* been able to find the convoy proper instead of just a straggler, the devastation could have been total.

The February 8–10 battle with HG-53 was the prototype of how Doenitz wanted to conduct convoy attacks in the months ahead. By striking with a

Above: An Allied escort prosecutes a submarine contact. By early 1941, the British began to equip their ships with better sensor systems, including radar, which made U-boat night surface attacks on convoys much more difficult than in the fall of 1940. Left: To help combat night surface attacks, the Allies armed their merchant ships. Here, a 5-inch gun crew sends shells down range.

Above: The skill and courage displayed by the U-boat crews continued to net results, even as their own losses mounted. *Below:* In January 1941, the Luftwaffe began to support U-boat operations with long-range reconnaissance/bombing missions with KG-40's small force of Fw-200 Kondors. These four-engine aircraft had been built as prewar airliners.

An Allied escort riding the heavy Atlantic seas. At times, even the most seasoned sailors grew seasick as their vessels tossed about.

three-dimensional force, the Kriegsmarine could overwhelm the Allied convoy defenses.

Doenitz's new offensive started with a string of brutal, one-sided German victories. After the HG-53 battle, the Kondors spotted convoy OB-288 near the Faroe Islands. Subsequent attacks by KG-40 damaged two ships. U-boats claimed three more that night. The convoy had no escort and was helpless before this round-the-clock onslaught. The following night, a pack of five U-boats and an Italian sub waded into the fray and destroyed ten more ships.

While the U-boats and Kondors savaged OB-288, OB-289 sailed right into *U-552*'s path near the Faroes. The Germans struck gold, and Doenitz ordered the three nearest U-boats to attack the convoy. Kapitänleutnant Udo Heilmann, skipper of *U-97*, found OB-289 and sank three merchant ships.

In forty-eight hours, the British had lost thirteen ships to sub and air attack in the Atlantic.

The following day, February 25, 1941, Gunter Prien discovered OB-290. The British had tried to reroute the convoy south of the slaughter engulfing OB-288 and 289, a move that sent OB-290 directly into the path of Germany's premier U-boat skipper. Prien sent two ships to the bottom that night. On the twenty-sixth, the Kondors supplied the second blow when they blew seven ships out of the water. It was the highest single-day total KG-40 would score in the Atlantic during World War II.

Three consecutive convoys had taken significant losses. To the merchant seamen risking their lives on

A typical depth-charge attack created a spectacle few sailors would ever forget.

the Allied cause. He was one of the most cunning and tactically astute skippers under Doenitz's command.

On March 6, 1941, Prien discovered OB-293 and shadowed it. Doenitz ordered a wolf pack to attack the convoy, and soon Otto Kretschmer and Joachim Matz's *U-70*, a Type VIIC boat, gave chase some two hundred miles southeast of Iceland. Matz was the first to maneuver into an attack position. Shortly before dawn, Matz made his move. He missed one target, but damaged a cargo ship and the Dutch tanker *Mijdrecht*. Then to Matz's surprise, the tanker suddenly swung toward *U-70* and charged her. Before the Germans could maneuver clear of it, the Dutch tanker rammed the U-boat, inflicting extensive damage. Matz ordered the boat down, but as they descended, the sub began shipping water. Matz found it increasingly difficult to maintain depth as the amount of water entering the sub grew.

Meanwhile on the surface, two British escorts arrived. Pinging the area around *U-70* with their ASDICS, the corvettes HMS *Arbutus* and HMS *Camelia* gradually zeroed in on their quarry. Matz tried to creep away from the two corvettes without luck. The two escorts made repeated runs on ASDIC contacts, dropping almost a hundred depth. During one depth charge attack, the *U-70*'s crew lost control of their boat and it plunged below 650 feet. In desperation, the Germans blew their tanks and the crippled sub shot to the surface, where the waiting corvettes pounded it with gunfire until the crew abandoned ship. About half the crew, including Matz, survived and were picked up by the *Arbutus* and *Camelia*. The Atlantic claimed the others.

About the same time *U-70* launched its initial attack, Prien took aim at a 20,638-ton British whaling ship. The *Terje Viken* was actually a German-built vessel, having been launched in 1936 at the Deschimag Werk Weser yard in Bremen. Delivered to the United Whalers LTD in London, the vessel had been plying the Atlantic for almost two years in service of the Allied cause. She proved to be a tempting target due to her size.

Two of Prien's torpedoes struck the whaler just after 0500 on March 7. Crippled but still afloat, she soon attracted *U-70*'s attention, but Matz's three-torpedo spread went wide of its mark at 0550. At that moment, Otto Kretschmer sent two eels toward her, both of which

wheezing old cargo ships, it must have seemed like nothing was getting across the Atlantic without running a gauntlet of air and submarine attacks.

All of this was the prelude to Doenitz's spring offensive. By the end of February, Doenitz's plan looked like it could deliver the deathblow to the British Empire. Yet, the Kriegsmarine's successes masked a number of developments within the Royal Navy, most of which came together in a confluence of tactical advances and technological breakthroughs in the following months.

Gunter Prien became the bell weather for this sudden change. After calling in the Kondors to feast on OB-290, Prien combed the Atlantic in search of more victims until he caught and destroyed the SS *Holmlea* and added 4,223 tons to his credit. This was his tenth patrol with *U-47*. His boat had sunk the battleship *Royal Oak* and thirty other ships representing almost 200,000 tons to

Above: A U-boat returns home after a long patrol. *Below:* A *Flower*-class corvette shepherds a convoy across the Atlantic. The *Flowers* were ordered during the 1939 and 1940 construction programs and signaled the Royal Navy's return to smaller escorts for convoy protection. Capable of sixteen knots, they carried a 4-inch gun, depth charges, and ASDIC. A total of 267 were built.

An aerial attack on a surfaced U-boat in the Atlantic.

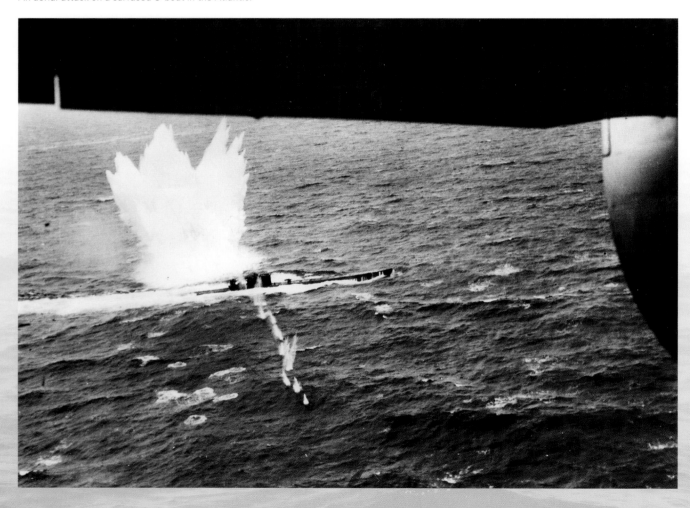

An Allied sailor prepares to launch depth charges against a German U-boat on a spray-swept deck in heavy seas. Such were the features of this aquatic battlefield.

struck her port side. She slowly capsized and sank a week later. The *Terje Viken* became one of the largest merchant ships to be sunk by the Germans during World War II. She was also Gunther Prien's last victim.

Exactly what happened to *U-47* remains shrouded in the chaos of this engagement. As the convoy's escorts swept down on the U-boats in the area, the German aces dove and scattered. The Royal Navy hunted them down with ruthless precision. Matz in *U-70* succumbed first. Then HMS *Wolverine* found a sub on the surface and drove it deep. *Wolverine* launched repeated depth-charge attacks over the next four hours. At one point, the sub suddenly surfaced so close to the British warship that her main guns could not be brought to bear on it. Seconds later, the U-boat dipped beneath the waves, only to have *Wolverine* lace the water with more depth charges.

Eyewitnesses aboard *Wolverine* saw an enormous underwater flash behind their vessel. Flames shot straight out of the water, haloed with an eerie subsurface orange glow. When it faded, the Atlantic swells were peppered with debris.

Most postwar accounts believe *Wolverine* sank *U-47* in that attack. Otto Kretschmer later suggested that one of Prien's own torpedoes went rogue, circled back after being fired, and struck *U-47* a fatal blow. Postwar scholarship indicates that *Wolverine* may have attacked U-boat UA, a sub built for the Turkish Navy and taken over by the Kriegsmarine at the start of the war. It survived a depth charge attack during the OB-293 convoy battle, but there is no way to ascertain the truth. However it happened, Gunter Prien and his crew died in action that night. Churchill announced the ace's death before the Germans did, taunting the Nazis who had not acknowledged their hero's loss. It was not until May that Berlin officially admitted Prien had died in battle.

Above left: Sending a line across to an antisubmarine warfare escort. Inter-ship communications were almost always a challenge in the rough North Atlantic. *Above right:* A badly damaged U-boat limps home after a fierce engagement in the Atlantic.

After the war, rumors surfaced that Prien did not die in the Atlantic. Instead, they suggested that he had refused to take *U-47* out on patrol, as he felt it was mechanically unreliable. His act of mutiny cost him his command, and, according to these rumors, he was sent to a concentration camp. The Nazi's could not court martial their media icon, so he vanished into the camp system and was executed in early 1945.

Variations of this story have appeared for decades, but there has yet to be any substantive evidence to show that Prien died anywhere other than with his men aboard the same gray wolf he guided into Scapa Flow at the outbreak of the war.

However it happened, Germany had lost the face of the U-boat fleet. Prien had become a symbol, not only to his fellow submariners, but also to the German forces. Daring, cocky, and devoted to the Nazi cause, Prien was the perfect hero for the tightly controlled German media machine. His death was a body blow to the Kriegsmarine's morale.

Yet the war stopped for no hero, no ace. A week after Prien's death, *U-110* spotted convoy HX-112 inbound for England southeast of Iceland. Fritz-Julius Lemp, with seventeen ships to his credit, had taken command of this old prewar Type IXB boat after leaving *U-30* in November 1940.

Lemp stalked the convoy and maneuvered for a shot. Shortly after midnight, he gained a good solution and ordered his crew to launch a spread of eels.

Convoy HX-112 was well protected by a group of Royal Navy antisubmarine warfare (ASW) vessels known as Escort Group 5. Led by Cmdr. Donald Macintyre, the screen for the fifty ships in HX-112 consisted of seven antisubmarine warfare vessels, including the destroyers HMS *Walker*, *Vanoc*, *Volunteer*, *Sardonyx*, and *Scimitar*, plus two *Flower*-class corvettes. Escort Group 5 was

Above: Alles Kaputt was a renamed Junkers Ju 290 which was surrendered to the Army Air Forces at the end of the war with Germany in May 1945. It was a popular attraction at U.S. air shows throughout 1946 but was scrapped at the end of the year. (In the foreground is a Japanese Ohka, a kamikaze-piloted flying bomb.) *Below:* A Kondor attacks an Allied merchant ship. The first half of 1941 saw the Focke-Wulf Fw-200s of KG-40 sink dozens of vessels, prompting Churchill to call them the "scourge of the Atlantic."

Hitler attends the launching of Germany's most formidable battleship: the *Bismarck*. When she was completed, the British had nothing capable of matching it one on one. The Royal Navy's only hope was to use its superior numbers to bring her to bay.

one of the first attempts to set up an integrated ASW team that would train and fight together in the months ahead. The Royal Navy had studied the lessons of the previous year and had concluded closer coordination between escorts was a key to better protection of the convoys. After Lemp discovered HX-112, that theory would be put to the test.

Macintyre stood on the bridge of HMS *Walker* in the early hours of March 16, watching the convoy pitch and roll through the dark swells. Born in 1904, he joined the Royal Navy in 1926 and became an aviator. After serving aboard the carriers *Hermes* and *Furious*, Macintyre left the Fleet Air Army in 1935 to take command of his first ship, HMS *Kingfisher*. In 1940, he fought in the Norwegian campaign, and at Narvik, while skippering the destroyer HMS *Hesperus*. Following the Allied withdrawal, Macintyre spent the next year at sea covering convoys in the Atlantic. Experienced, astute, and very capable, Macintyre was a humble man and an inspiring leader. Those assets made him a natural choice to take command of Escort Group 5.

While on *Walker*'s bridge, Macintyre found himself with a front-row seat to Lemp's attack on HX-112. One of his torpedoes struck the tanker SS *Erodona*. The torpedo detonated the oil tanks, lighting the night with a hellish glow.

In his memoirs, Macintyre recalled the scene: "I had never before seen this most appalling of all night disasters and on the bridge of *Walker* we were shocked into silence by the horror of it."

Escort Group 5 sprang into action, scouring the water around the convoy's flanks for the attacking sub, but Lemp crept away undetected. After a futile search, the corvette HMS *Bluebell* turned back to search for survivors from *Erodona*. Despite the explosion she had suffered, the vessel remained afloat. Half her crew had been immolated in the flames, but twenty-one men

were rescued. Miraculously, the tanker was later towed to Iceland, repaired, and returned to service in 1944.

The rest of the predawn hours passed in tense silence as all hands aboard HX-112's ships waited for the sickening thud of the next torpedo impact. With the sun came no relief from the tension. Said Macintyre, " . . . It seemed as though the shadow of impending doom hung above the convoy."

That shadow came in the form of the two leading aces in the U-boat arm: Schepke and Silent Otto Kretschmer. Together with *U-37* and *U-74*, the two aces stalked HX-112 throughout the day. The convoy lumbered on, bound for Liverpool with forty remaining ships. Most were tankers full of precious oil and aviation fuel.

As dusk approached, the tension mounted. The escorts kept a constant vigil on the convoy's flanks,

Rear Admiral Robert Burnett, who later commanded the cruiser squadron that helped sink *Scharnhorst*, stands at left with King George VI and Adm. John Tovey.

lookouts scanning the waves for the tell-tale stripe of white wake—surfaced U-boats left in their path.

Kretschmer was the first to strike. With *U-99* on the surface, Silent Otto slipped past Escort Group 5 and reached the port side of the convoy. The great ace had a field day. His crew blew five ships out of the water. The first, the Norwegian tanker *Ferm*, carried nine thousand tons of fuel oil. His second victim, the tanker *Beduin*, carried eleven thousand tons of petrol. The nineteen thousand tons dumped into the Atlantic from their shattered hulls represents an amount greater than the forty-sixth largest oil spill in peacetime history, 1991's Kirki tanker disaster off the southwest coast of Australia. Kretschmer also sank the SS *Venentia* that night, which carried seven thousand tons of maize. The next morning, the Atlantic was covered with oil-soaked debris, bodies, and corn bobbing in the swells. Such were the battlefields of the tonnage war.

As ships exploded and went down, Macintyre grew frantic. He sent his warships on zig-zag arcs on the convoy's perimeter in hopes of finding the attacking U-boats. He later wrote, "I was near to despair and racked my brains to find some way to stop the holocaust."

Twice his warships spotted surfaced U-boats and rushed to depth charge them. The second time, MacIntyre thought his men had hit the sub after it crash-dived, but he was not convinced it had been destroyed. Thirty minutes later, his ASDIC operator reacquired contact with the boat. Macintyre called in *Vanoc* to help out, and both destroyers made repeated depth-charge runs until the water was so disturbed that the ASDIC sensors aboard both ships were rendered useless. Macintyre decided to rescue the crew of the SS *JB White* while Lt. Cmdr. P. R. Ward's *Vanoc* covered him.

After *Walker* pulled the last seaman from the water, *Vanoc* charged off into the night. Communication between *Walker* and *Vanoc* broke down, and Macintyre didn't realize that *Vanoc* had detected a surfaced U-boat with her brand new Type 286M radar array. This was the first time such a system had detected a surfaced submarine, but it was a sign of what was to come. The days of U-boats attacking convoys on the surface were numbered.

Vanoc had spotted *U-100*, the submerged submarine that she and *Walker* were tag teaming. Schepke saw the destroyer and sensed that she intended to ram his boat. Watching *Vanoc* from his periscope, one of his men heard him say that the destroyer was going to miss them astern.

Seconds later, *Vanoc*'s bow tore through *U-100*'s hull and crushed Joachim Schepke against the periscope.

The Type VIIB sank so quickly that only six of Schepke's men were able to escape.

Nearby, Otto Kretschmer had expended his torpedoes and was heading for home. Believing they were out of danger, he turned the boat over to his officer of the watch and went below. It proved to be a poor decision. Kretschmer's watch officer spotted either *Vanoc* or *Walker* and rashly ordered a crash dive against Silent Otto's standing orders. The standard tactic in such a situation was to turn away from the threat and try to escape on the surface. Diving just put the boat within the British ASDIC performance envelope.

Sure enough Macintyre's operator picked up *U-99*. *Walker* sped to the scene and laid a pattern of six depth charges so accurately that it crippled Kretschmer's boat.

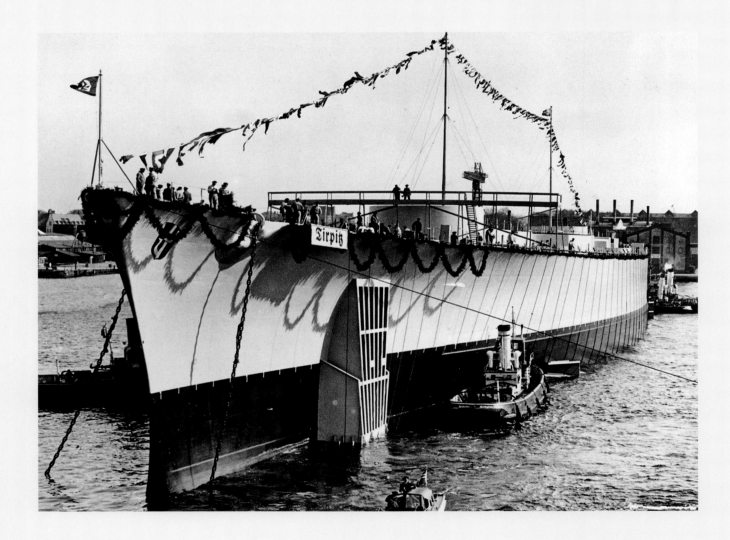

Above: HMS *Victorious* at sea with a deck load of Sea Hurricanes and Fairey Albacore torpedo bombers. *Victorious's* airmen scored a torpedo hit on *Bismarck* and reduced her top speed to sixteen knots and gave the Home Fleet a chance to catch the elusive battleship. *Opposite:* After *Bismarck* was hunted down, *Tirpitz* became the biggest remaining surface threat to Allied convoys. She was relentlessly attacked by air and by special operations until finally destroyed in November 1944.

The sub plunged to 720 feet before the Germans got it under control. The hull began to leak and the boat's electric motors had been knocked out, as had her steering gear. Kretschmer could not escape. He ordered *U-99* to the surface. *Vanoc* speared the German sub with her searchlight the moment she broke the surface. Astern of *Walker*, *U-99* had no chance against two destroyers.

Both warships poured gunfire at the U-boat, most of it ineffectual, but the display convinced Kretschmer to surrender. He signaled his enemies with a blinker light: "We are sinking." He asked the British to save his crew. Just before leaving his command, Kretschmer radioed Doenitz's headquarters and reported his final attacks. Then, he joined his crew in the water.

Walker picked up all but three of *U-99*'s crew, which made for some tense initial moments as the survivors of the *JB White* were also on board. Kretschmer was the last man fished out of the ocean with his pair of

custom-made Zeiss binoculars Doenitz had presented to his top aces. Macintyre liberated them and wore them every day he was at sea until the war's end.

Germany had lost her three most capable U-boat aces. Schepke went to his death aboard *U-100* with thirty-seven ships and 155,000 tons to his credit. Kretschmer entered Allied captivity as the leading ace of the war: forty-six ships and 273,000 tons. He was known as the "Tonnage King," and his record was never surpassed, though Wolfgang Lueth ultimately equaled his forty-six-ship total.

It was a devastating blow to the U-boat arm. In three weeks, Doenitz's spring offensive had cost him five boats, which after the scant losses in 1940 sent shock waves through the U-boat force. In retrospect, the death of Prien and Schepke, plus the loss of Silent Otto, signaled the end of "The Happy Time." The days of easy pickings in the North Atlantic were over.

Above: Despite the Fleet Air Arm's obsolete aircraft and shrinking number of available decks from which to operate, the brave British naval aviators scored several striking victories during the war, including crippling the *Bismarck* and sinking the Italian battle line in Taranto Harbor. *Below:* Force H hunting for the *Bismarck*: HMS *Renown* escorts *Ark Royal* in a photo taken from the cruiser *Sheffield*.

Though much hard fighting remained, a corner had been turned.

The Kriegsmarine's surface fleet learned the same lesson a few weeks later. On May 19, 1941, Admiral Luetjens sortied from Gotenhafen with the brand-new battleship *Bismarck* and the cruiser *Prinz Eugen* for Operation Rheinübung. Supported by four U-boats and a host of pre-positioned supply ships, Luetjens intended to reprise his raiding role in the North Atlantic.

Instead, the hunters became the hunted. After a stop in Norway, the *Bismarck* and *Prinz Eugen* tried to break into the North Atlantic via the Denmark Straits. The Royal Navy's surface screen detected and shadowed the Germans, which prompted HMS *Hood* and *Prince of Wales* to intercept them. The Bismarck outshot both British vessels and sent the Hood to the bottom with a magazine hit that killed all but three men. The *Prince of Wales*, which was suffering from severe mechanical failures in her main gun turrets, took repeated hits after the *Hood* went down. One of the *Bismark*'s shells passed through the bridge and wiped out the *Prince of Wales*'s command center, killing everyone there but the captain. Soon, only two of her ten 14-inch guns remained in action. Repeated hits by the Bismarck's 15-inch battery finally forced the *Prince of Wales* to retire. It was a striking tactical defeat, one of the worst the Royal Navy endured during the Atlantic War, but the Germans gained nothing from it.

After the engagement in the Denmark Straits, every available British warship converged on the North Atlantic in a desperate search for *Bismarck*. If the German battlewagon had been able to get into the convoy lanes, she had the firepower and speed to cause utter carnage.

Luetjens made it into the North Atlantic, but he did so with a badly damaged battleship. During the Denmark Straits engagement, the *Prince of Wales* managed to hit the *Bismarck* three times with 14-inch shells. Two of those hits tore open the *Bismarck*'s hull, causing a nine-degree list to port as she shipped more than two thousand tons of water. The forward fuel bunker was soon contaminated with sea water, and she ended up three degrees down by the bow with the additional weight. Worse, her crew discovered their battlewagon

Prince of Wales was damaged by the *Bismarck* shortly after the German battleship sank HMS *Hood*. *Prince of Wales* was later sunk by a Japanese air attack in December 1941. This photo was taken during that attack while maneuvering with HMS *Repulse*.

was leaking oil. With the Royal Navy in hot pursuit, this was akin to leaving a trail of breadcrumbs behind her for the enemy to follow. Indeed, a searching Sunderland spotted Bismarck's oil slick, which the Coastal Command aviators reported to two cruisers trying to find and shadow the German ships.

Luetjens had the most modern, technologically advanced battleship in the world at that time within reach of the British convoy lanes, but thanks to those three shells, the ship was in no position to carry out her mission. He elected to turn for the Bay of Biscay and

Three views of HMS *Hood*, the pride of the prewar British Navy. The huge battle cruiser displaced forty-six thousand tons, carried eight 15-inch guns, and could reach speeds in excess of twenty-eight knots.

put in at St. Nazaire, France, for repairs. Meanwhile, he intended to cut the *Prinz Eugen* loose to conduct commerce raiding operations.

The British hunted the *Bismarck* with unrelenting determination, driven by a frantic Churchill who had ordered her sunk at all costs. When the Royal Navy's Home Fleet began to run low on fuel, Churchill suggested continuing the chase until its destroyers emptied their oil bunkers and were taken under tow by the fleet's battleships. The idea was ridiculous, but the intent behind it was not: the prime minister wanted *Bismarck* destroyed.

By the morning of May 25, 1941, it looked like Luetjens would escape to France. The Home Fleet was steaming at full speed, but its battleships did not have the capability to keep pace with the *Bismarck*'s thirty-knot max speed.

Admiral John Tovey, commander of the Home Fleet, decided to roll the dice. At 1600 on May 25, 1941, he sent HMS *Victorious* ahead of his surface force with a light screen of cruisers in hopes that the aircraft carrier could get close enough to launch her air group against *Bismarck*.

At 2200, nine Fairy Swordfish biplane bombers waddled off *Victorious*'s heaving deck. In the twilight, the "Stringbag" pilots almost attacked one of the Royal Navy cruisers shadowing *Bismarck*. Fortunately, they realized their mistake in the nick of time and banked for the real target several miles ahead.

Battling through fierce, but inaccurate antiaircraft fire, the Swordfish crews dropped their torpedoes and escaped without loss. *Bismarck* maneuvered radically and evaded eight of the fish. But one exploded against

(continued on page 136)

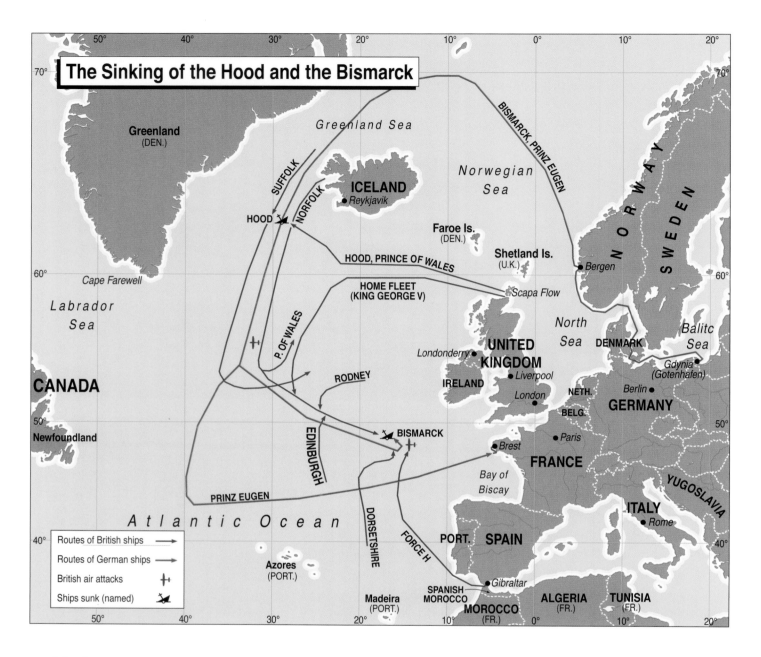

The Sinking of the Hood and the Bismarck

Greenland
(DEN.)

Greenland Sea

ICELAND
• Reykjavik

SUFFOLK

NORFOLK

HOOD

BISMARCK, PRINZ EUGEN

Norwegian Sea

Faroe Is.
(DEN.)

Shetland Is.
(U.K.)

• Bergen

N O R W A Y

S W E D E N

HOOD, PRINCE OF WALES

HOME FLEET
(KING GEORGE V)

Scapa Flow

Cape Farewell

Labrador Sea

P. OF WALES

North Sea

DENMARK

Baltic Sea

Gdynia
(Gotenhafen)

Londonderry

UNITED KINGDOM

CANADA

RODNEY

IRELAND

• Liverpool

London

NETH.
BELG.

Berlin •

GERMANY

Newfoundland

EDINBURGH

BISMARCK

• Brest

• Paris

FRANCE

YUGOSLAVIA

PRINZ EUGEN

Bay of Biscay

ITALY
• Rome

A t l a n t i c   O c e a n

DORSETSHIRE

FORCE H

Azores
(PORT.)

PORT.

SPAIN

Routes of British ships	
Routes of German ships	
British air attacks	
Ships sunk (named)	

Madeira
(PORT.)

SPANISH MOROCCO

• Gibraltar

MOROCCO
(FR.)

ALGERIA
(FR.)

TUNISIA
(FR.)

Below: Commissioned in 1920, the *Hood* entered World War II outgunned by many German vessels, but there was no time to upgrade the battlecruiser. On May 24, 1941, the *Hood*'s aft magazine exploded after the ship was fired upon by the *Bismarck*. The *Hood* sunk in three minutes with only three survivors. *The-Blueprints.com*

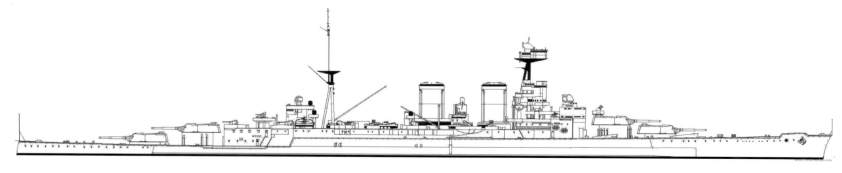

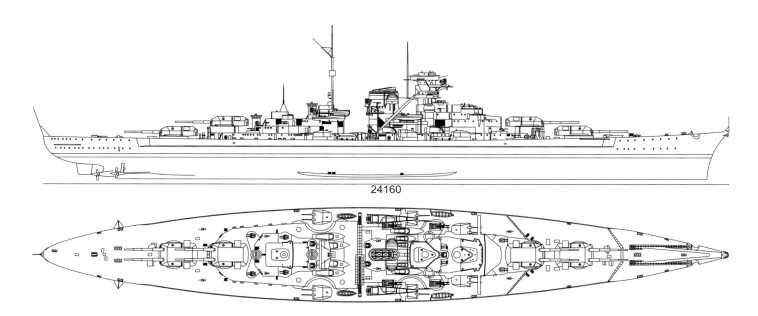

24160

Above: The Bismarck and sister ship Tirpitz were Germany's largest battleships of the war. Following Bismarck's sinking of the Hood, the British made sinking the Bismarck a priority. The-Blueprints.com Below: Early on May 27, 1941, HMS King George V (pictured), accompanied by a second battleship, Rodney, opened fire on the Bismarck. Their attack continued until they were nearly out of ammo and fuel. Bismarck was still afloat, but defenseless and low in the water. The Hood was avenged. The-Blueprints.com

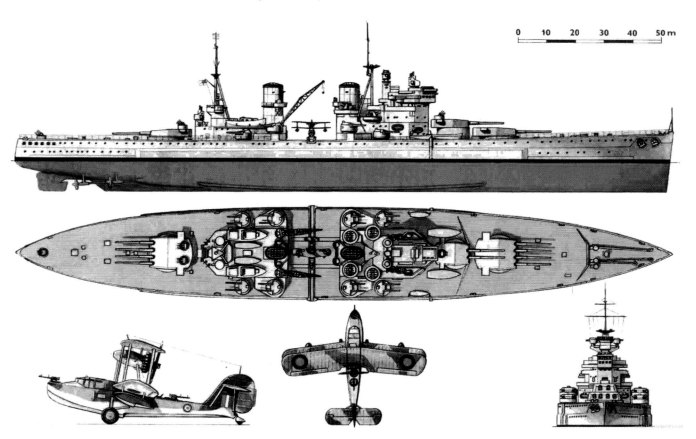

(continued from page 132)

her main belt armor. The concussion wave was so fierce that it blew a nearby sailor against a bulkhead and killed him.

At first it looked like the attack had failed. But as the Swordfish disappeared into the growing darkness, *Bismarck*'s speed fell off. The severe maneuvers used to evade the other torpedoes had caused more flooding below decks from the *Prince of Wales*' shell hits. As some of the temporary repairs failed under the stress, one of the *Bismarck*'s portside boiler rooms flooded, reducing speed to a mere sixteen knots.

The Germans furiously effected repairs, but time was running against Luetjens. At the same time, the fuel situation facing the British became critical. Several key warships, including *Victorious* and *Prince of Wales*, had to abandon the pursuit. Several other ships, including the new battleship *King George V,* were approaching the point where they would not be able to make it back to a friendly port if they stayed in the hunt. The situation was getting desperate for the Royal Navy, but Churchill refused to let up. He sent Tovey a message that read in part, "*Bismarck* must be sunk at all costs, even if it means towing *King George V.*"

That night, the *Bismarck* managed to shake loose from the Royal Navy cruisers shadowing her. Luetjens looped around the British and sent them scurrying to reacquire the pursuit. By now, the German admiral intended to make for Brest instead of St. Nazaire, and for a few hours on the twenty-sixth, it looked like he would pull it off.

That morning, though, a Consolidated PBY Catalina flying boat, flown by a U.S. Navy ensign, spotted *Bismarck* about eight miles northwest of Brest. The British still had a chance.

To support the Home Fleet's chase, the Admiralty had ordered Force H into the Atlantic a few days before. Until then, Force H had been fighting in the Mediterranean Sea from its base at Gibraltar. Composed of the aircraft carrier *Ark Royal*, battle cruiser *Renown*, and the light cruiser *Sheffield*, Force H changed the pursuit entirely.

With the *Bismarck* located, the *Ark Royal* launched its air group against her. Once more, a Fleet Air Arm

Opposite above: The *Bismark* fires on the *Prince of Wales* near the end of the Battle of the Denmark Strait. The *Hood* has already sunk. *Opposite below:* King George V at anchor in Iceland. She fired 335 shells from her main battery at the *Bismarck* during the final battle with the German warship in May 1941.

Swordfish squadron lumbered into the fray—and attacked the British cruiser *Sheffield*. All the torpedoes missed.

A second strike was launched that evening. Fifteen Swordfish piled onto the *Bismarck*. Two torpedoes found the mark. One struck the belt armor again, doing minor flooding damage. But the second one exploded on the stern beside the port rudder shaft. The blast crippled *Bismarck*, jamming her steering and sending her in a wide series of circles.

The crew worked feverishly but could not regain control over their vessel. Admiral Tovey's ships had the time they needed. He sent five destroyers to harass the Germans throughout the night, launching star shells and torpedoes. The destroyers failed to score any hits, but they wore out the *Bismarck*'s crew. By dawn, when Tovey's main force closed for the killing blow, the Germans' morale had collapsed.

As the sun came up on the twenty-seventh, the main battle was joined. This time, it was a one-sided contest. Leading the fight for the British was the *King George V,* now perilously short of fuel, plus the battleship *Rodney* and two heavy cruisers.

The fight raged through the morning. Just after 0900, a 16-inch shell from HMS *Rodney* tore through *Bismarck*'s forward superstructure, crippling the forward main gun turrets and killing hundreds of men. Luetjens and the *Bismarck*'s captain were among those who perished in the catastrophic blast.

The ship fought on, her remaining guns in local control. The two Royal Navy battlewagons poured more than seven hundred main gun rounds into the dying German ship. At 1000, the *Rodney* closed to point-blank range to fire torpedoes and deliver the coup de grace. As scores of shell strikes transformed *Bismarck* into a fiery inferno, the shattered crew abandoned ship. About then, one of the Royal Navy cruisers scored two torpedo hits that finished off the German warship. *Bismarck* turned

Opposite and above: The Fairey Swordfish, an obsolete throwback from the age of fabric-covered biplanes, performed superbly in the heavy Atlantic seas. During the hunt for the *Bismarck*, two key torpedo hits by Swordfish crews turned the chase in the Royal Navy's favor.

turtle and sank by the stern as a pitiful few survivors struggled in the water around her. Of the 2,100 men aboard when she left Germany nine days before, only 114 survived this final battle.

Churchill had his victory. The latest and most advanced battleship on the planet had been hunted down and destroyed, which in itself was a huge propaganda victory. More important, the convoy lanes had been secured. Never again would Admiral Raeder attempt

to send surface raiders into the North Atlantic. The *Bismarck*'s loss soured Hitler on his fleet, an attitude that only worsened in the year ahead. Raeder's stock, never high at Hitler's headquarters, plummeted.

The twin defeats derailed the German spring offensive. As if this wasn't enough, the British inflicted one more critical strategic defeat on their enemies with a brilliant coup that spring.

Since sinking the *Athenia* at the outset of the war,

Fritz-Julius Lemp became yet another of Germany's vaunted U-boat aces to be killed in the Atlantic during the fighting in the spring of 1941. Before his submarine sank, the British recovered the sub's Enigma machine, a major coup in the code-breaking war.

Fritz-Julius Lemp had gone on to sink seventeen more ships while commanding *U-30*. In 1939, his crew had crippled the British battleship *Barham*. For this and other feats, he'd become the seventh U-boat ace to be awarded the coveted Knights Cross. In November 1940, he was transferred to command *U-110*, a new Type IXB that he spent the winter of 1940–41 working up in the Baltic. He sortied her from Kiel in March 1941 on her maiden combat patrol (it was Lemp's ninth), but the crew found few targets and put in at Lorient with only two ships sunk. Worse, at the end of March, while running on the surface, Lemp deployed his deck gun crew. As they fired their 105mm cannon, it malfunctioned and exploded, killing the three men.

Hoping for better luck, Lemp took *U-110* back out to sea in mid-April. On May 9, 1941, he launched a submerged attack on convoy OB-116 south of Iceland. After a torpedo malfunction, the *U-110*'s periscope was detected by nearby escorts. The corvette HMS *Aubretia* swept toward the submarine and laid a well-placed pattern of depth charges. Lemp's crew took a beating in this attack. While the *U-110* tried to slip away, two more escorts raced to the scene and pummeled the U-boat with more depth charges. This second round crippled Lemp's boat and he had no choice but to surface.

He blew his tanks and *U-110* appeared right in front of the B-class destroyer HMS *Bulldog* and the HMS *Broadway*. The latter was a flush deck destroyer given to the Royal Navy by the United States.

Facing two well-armed tin cans spelled *U-110*'s doom. Lemp ordered his men to abandon ship, but as they streamed out of the boat's hatches, the British thought the Germans meant to fight it out. The destroyers opened fire, raking the crew with cannon and machine gunfire. Many of the U-boat men drowned or were killed by the gunfire until the Brits finally realized they

The Allies captured or boarded several other U-boats. The American seizure of *U-505* remains the most famous, but the British also seized *U-570* (seen here with HMS *Burwell*, one of the World War I—era destroyers the United States gave to Britain in the Destroyer for Bases Agreement). *U-570* became the only U-boat to serve on operational patrols for both sides during the war.

were simply trying to escape. They ceased fire and HMS *Bulldog* made to ram *U-110* to finish her off. At the last minute, her commander intuited that they might be able to capture the boat instead.

He hove to, and as the German survivors were pulled out of the water, a boarding party set off toward *U-110*. Meanwhile, Lemp had ended up in the rolling swells with the rest of his men. As the *Bulldog* approached, he realized his boat could fall into enemy hands. He began swimming back to it, and that was the last his crew saw of him. Whether he was killed by the boarding party or drowned is unknown. Whatever the case, the boarding party climbed onto *U-110* and secured her.

Not only did the British score a U-boat out of this engagement, but they captured a complete Enigma code machine with the Officers Only setting on it. They also bagged the Short Signals Code, known as *Kurzsignale*, which was designed to send burst transmissions of short duration so that British direction finders could not zero in on the U-boat's location.

Seizing *U-110* was one of the pivotal moments of the code war. It was kept so secret that Lemp's crew didn't even know their vessel had fallen into British hands. The crippled boat was taken under tow toward Iceland, but eventually sank en route. No matter. The damage had been done. The Enigma, codes, and ciphers all arrived at Bletchley Park, where they were instrumental in ensuring the Kriegsmarine's signal traffic could be decoded and read by the British through the rest of 1941.

In two months, the Royal Navy had managed to beat back the Kriegsmarine's triple threat. Thanks to the *Bismarck* debacle, the German surface fleet would never again be a factor in the North Atlantic. The U-boat force had been dealt stinging defeats, forcing Doenitz to temporarily abandon the North Atlantic. The British dealt a third blow to the Germans and their antishipping Kondor group that had wrought so much havoc on the convoys earlier in the year.

Fighter cover was the way to combat marauding four engined bombers. The Royal Navy's few remaining carriers were already committed elsewhere, and escort carriers had yet to enter service. Those baby flat-tops were coming, but until they could be deployed in numbers, the Royal Navy came up with a unique stop gap called the CAM (catapult armed merchant) ship.

The idea behind these vessels was indicative of both British creativity and their desperation. About three dozen cargo ships were taken into the program and modified with catapults on their bows. Atop the catapult sat a navalized Hawker Hurricane fighter, piloted by a volunteer aviator. The Royal Navy planned to escort convoys with one or two CAM ships, depending on the threat level from Kondors. When inbound German aircraft were detected, the Hurricane pilot would launch from the catapult to intercept.

Of course, there was a problem here. Without a deck to land on following the mission, the Hurricane pilot would either have to ditch alongside a vessel in the convoy or bail out, hoping he didn't drown before he could free himself from his parachute. All fifty pilots in the program volunteered to do this.

The first two CAM ships went operational at the end of May 1941. One of them was promptly sunk by *U-118*, but more soon joined the fight. The first CAM-launched Sea Hurricane kill over a Condor took place in August 1941. Others soon followed.

HMS *Audacity*, the first escort carrier to be deployed by the Royal Navy, protected her first convoy in September. Her arrival, plus the CAM ships, signaled an end to the Kondor Scourge. *Audacity*'s Grumman Martlet fighters shot down seven Fw-200s during the course of three convoy missions. They also played the key role in crippling *U-131* in December.

Through 1941, KG-40 possessed only handful of Kondors. Such losses could not be sustained. Their attacks in the North Atlantic ceased, and KG-40's Focke-Wulfs were ordered to function exclusively in the long-range maritime reconnaissance role.

The year started with great promise for the German side, but the sailors, submariners, and aviators of the Third Reich soon discovered the one-sided days of 1940 had given way to a brutal, pitched battle against an aggressive and adaptable foe. With their backs to the wall and defeat seemingly on the horizon, the British had made hard changes and added new weapons, tactics, and ships to the battle. Combined with the skill and courage of the Royal Navy's sailors, the changes had worked. Britain would survive.

THE ULTRA SECRET

Invented by German engineer Arthur Scherbius at the end of World War I, the electromechanical Enigma cipher machine was first used by private corporations to prevent industrial espionage. In 1925, the German navy adopted it, and the army soon followed suit.

In 1932, while working in the Polish Cipher Bureau, the young mathematician Marian Rejewski was assigned to decrypt Germany's Enigma traffic. Considered one of history's greatest cryptologists, Rejewski succeeded where others failed, deducing the secret internal wiring of the machine in only a couple of weeks. After that breakthrough, Rejewski's team successfully decrypted German military signals for the next six years. In 1938, the Germans increased the number of rotor combinations in their Enigmas and the Poles' source of information dried up.

Just before the 1939 German invasion, the Poles handed over all their equipment and expertise to the British and French. With this assistance, the Allies were able to score one of history's greatest intelligence coups.

The code-breaking effort was centered outside of London at the Bletchley Park complex. There, the initial team grew from thirty to several thousand quirky, brilliant specialists. Bletchley became home to cryptologists, linguists, German scholars, mathematicians, and at least one Olympic chess player.

All the brainpower in the world wouldn't crack the Enigma alone. The British needed the latest version of the German machine, so they executed a series special operations designed to capture one. The Royal Navy targeted German weather ships operating in the North Atlantic and captured two of them in 1941. Both provided a gold mine of data for Bletchley, but the most important coup came when Fritz-Julius Lemp's *U-110* was captured in an unplanned engagement in May 1941. Aboard Lemp's boat, the Royal Navy boarding party snared an Enigma and all the latest codebooks.

Those successes, combined with the tireless efforts at Bletchley, led to key breakthroughs. The British broke the German naval Enigma code and that summer could read most of Doenitz's communication with his boats in the Atlantic. That allowed the Allies to route their convoys around the murderous wolf packs.

On February 1, 1942, the German U-boat fleet adopted a new, four-rotor Enigma, along a new key known as Shark. The change blinded the Allies at a critical moment in the Atlantic, and losses skyrocketed as Doenitz's subs preyed on the American coastal shipping lanes.

Hundreds of thousands of military and civilian lives depended on Bletchley Park breaking the new codes for the U-boats. Aiding the effort were the Germans themselves, who refused to believe their code could be compromised. Doenitz's controlling command also required so much radio communication between his headquarters and his boats that Bletchley Park had an abundance of traffic with which to search for patterns that could help speed the code-breaking process.

On October 30, 1942, the Royal Navy boarded crippled *U-559* and captured the equipment and codebooks needed to break the Shark key. The future father of computer science, Alan Turing, is largely credited with that break, which took place in December 1942. That was the crucial moment in the code war, as it intersected with the final, greatest battles in the North Atlantic. The Allies, blinded for so long, could once again pinpoint the exact location of Doenitz's boats. Instead of just trying to avoid them by rerouting convoys, the Allies now had the power to attack these boats with hunter-killer groups of escorts and aircraft carriers. The Allies, so long on the defensive in the Atlantic, took the war directly to Doenitz's wolves. Thanks to Bletchley Park, the 1943 offensive swept the North Atlantic clean of U-boats and secured victory in the convoy war.

—*Allison Serventi Morgan*

CHAPTER EIGHT

THE UNDECLARED WAR

When war broke out in 1939, the American people wanted nothing to do with it. Two decades of soul-searching bitterness over World War I had left the country in a hermitlike mood. Congress reflected that sentiment and passed a series of laws dubbed the Neutrality Acts. The Neutrality Acts banned arms sales to warring nations and stated that American citizens traveling to war zones would do so at their own risk. In 1939, another bill amended the initial one to allow for arms sales to warring nations on a "cash and carry" basis. This was supposed to prevent American banks, or the federal government, from extending credit to a foreign power, which was widely considered to be one of the reasons why America was dragged into World War I.

Through 1940, President Franklin Roosevelt pushed for a more active role against Germany. The fall of France and plight of the British prompted FDR to take action, which sparked considerable controversy at home for him.

On September 2, 1940, the Destroyer for Bases Agreement was signed, giving the United States access to Commonwealth possessions in the Western Hemisphere so air and naval bases could be developed by the United States. This included land in Newfoundland, Bermuda, and several islands in the Caribbean. In return, FDR gave Churchill the fifty World War I–era destroyers he'd been asking for through the summer.

It was a great deal for the United States, whose eastern ramparts would be greatly strengthened when the bases were operational. The Brits, including Churchill, felt they got the short end of the stick, but given their circumstances they had little choice but to agree to the deal.

The United States handed over the fifty World War I–era flush deck destroyers that fall. Twenty years of neglect in mothballs left them in poor condition, and each one required considerable work to become operational. As they joined the Royal Navy, the Brits found them poorly suited for Atlantic operations. With their low superstructure, they were wet ships, making the crews miserable in rough seas. Beggars, however, could not be choosers. The ships were thrown into the fray.

Whatever their shortcomings, the addition of fifty escorts came at a vital time when the British desperately needed antisubmarine warfare (ASW) vessels. Plus, the deal served as the first step toward outright American involvement in the war.

Opposite: In September 1940, the United States took its first step toward supporting the British war effort with the Destroyer for Bases Agreement. As part of the agreement, the Royal Navy received fifty World War I–era *Flush Deck*- and *Clemson*-class destroyers like this one, USS *John Francis Burnes*.

USS *New York* served as one of the U.S. Navy's deterrents to German aggression in the Atlantic. She took part in the Neutrality Patrols and later convoy escort operations.

As the British fought alone that winter, their cash reserves ran low. Without U.S. weapons they could not sustain their war effort, yet the cash and carry system threatened to bankrupt the British. Roosevelt worked to solve the crisis. In December 1940, he announced that the United States would become the "arsenal of democracy," by providing the Allies with the arms and supplies they needed. The speech generated howls from isolationists, but it led to one of the twentieth-century's pivotal congressional moments a few months later.

In early 1941, the Democrats introduced a bill called An Act to Further Promote the Defense of the United States. Popularly known as the Lend-Lease bill, it authorized the U.S. government to loan or give military supplies to the Allies. Initially, this included only Britain, Canada, and the Free French, but it was later extended to include the Soviet Union and China.

The bill created a firestorm of protest by isolationists, Republicans, and antiwar Democrats. Through February, as debate polarized the country, Roosevelt threw all his folksy charm behind the bill. At a press conference the president likened Lend-Lease to helping a neighbor whose house had caught fire and needed to borrow a hose to extinguish the blaze.

"What do I do in such a crisis? I don't say, 'Neighbor, my garden hose cost me fifteen dollars; you have to pay me fifteen dollars for it' . . . I don't want fifteen dollars —I want my garden hose back after the fire is over."

The analogy worked. A subsequent Gallup poll found that 54 percent of the country agreed with the president. On March 11, 1941, the Lend-Lease Act passed, paving the way for an eventual fifty billion dollars (more than half a trillion in today's currency) of war material to flow from U.S. shores to embattled nations around the globe.

The March vote presaged a much more active role in the war. In April, the navy issued OPPLAN-3-41, which instructed its captains to either drive off or attack any belligerent nation's vessels entering the Western Hemisphere if they did not have "West Indian possessions." This obviously meant the Germans and Italians, and the Western Hemisphere was defined to include everything from the Atlantic Ocean to the Azores. It meant that U.S. ships would inevitably end up battling U-boats.

Already, there had been isolated incidents between German U-boats and U.S. Navy vessels. On April 10, 1941, the U.S. destroyer *Niblack* had come across the survivors of a Dutch steamer sunk by a German U-boat off the Icelandic coast. Moments later, her sound operators detected a submerged contact, and the American destroyer depth charged it. It was the first time U.S. forces engaged an assumed German contact, though postwar research discovered there were no U-boats in that area at the time.

The following month, the SS *Robin Moor*, an American steamer, was stopped by *U-69* about seven hundred

(continued on page 151)

Above: The USS *New York* escorted the invasion force that carried the 6th Marine Division to Iceland in mid-1941. After that, the old battlewagon served as the station ship for Argentia, Newfoundland, before rejoining the transatlantic convoy operations in late 1941. *Below:* USS *Truxton* at sea before Pearl Harbor. A *Clemson*-class four piper, she joined the Atlantic Squadron in the spring of 1939 and took part in the Neutrality Patrols for the next two years. In late 1941, she began convoy escort duties in the North Atlantic, and she was lost in a massive gale off the coast of Newfoundland in February 1942. For much of 1941 and early 1942, the old four-piper destroyers played the leading role in the U.S. Navy's escort operations in the Atlantic.

Above: In 1941, as the war in the Atlantic drew the United States closer and closer to Great Britain, the U.S. Navy was forced to rely on old weapons and outdated ships to carry out FDR's orders to protect the sea lanes. *Below:* A Curtiss SOC-1 Seagull being catapulted off an American warship. Observation and light-bombing aircraft, the Seagulls were largely replaced by the Vought OS2U Kingfisher by early 1942. *Opposite:* The USS *Dahlgren* was another *Clemson*-class four piper that saw service during the war. She patrolled the Eastern Sea Frontier Atlantic until 1943.

Above left: During the war, food was strictly rationed in England. Such basics as butter, jam, eggs, and sugar—things most civilians took for granted before the war—became luxuries to the British people. The food supply in England was further tested in 1942 when hundreds of thousands of U.S. GIs began arriving and had to be fed as well. *Above right:* The threat of German raiders, such as *Scharnhorst* and *Tirpitz*, forced the U.S. Navy to keep a number of old battleships in the Atlantic to conduct convoy escort operations. Later, some of the newest American battleships to be built, including the USS *Washington*, saw service first in the Atlantic before deploying to the Pacific to face the Japanese navy. *Below:* The Latvian steamship SS *Ciltvaria*, seen here sinking off Cape Hatteras a month after the U.S. entry into the war.

The U.S. Navy's naval base at Guantanamo Bay, Cuba, seen in 1941. Gitmo's seaplanes and flying boats formed a crucial part of the antisubmarine effort in the Caribbean. Seen on the ramp are Consolidated PBY Catalinas, SOC Seagull floatplanes, and Sikorsky S-43 flying boats.

(continued from page 146)
miles west of Freetown, Sierra Leone. The Germans allowed the crew to board lifeboats, then sank *Robin Moor* with a torpedo and gunfire. The crew languished in the equatorial heat for two weeks before being rescued by passing vessels.

On May 27, 1941, Roosevelt declared a state of unlimited national emergency, after which the United States became directly involved in the Atlantic war. U.S. forces landed in Iceland and Greenland, where they established air and naval bases.

That summer, President Roosevelt and Winston Churchill met in person for the first time. Both secretly boarded warships that took them to Placentia Bay, Newfoundland, where the two great leaders crafted a vision of the future. What emerged became known as the Atlantic Charter, which became the foundation of the Anglo-American alliance. The charter included eight principles that included a declaration that the U.S. and Britain sought no territorial gain from the war. It also called for free trade, self-determination for the people of every nation to postwar disarmament, freedom of the seas, and the establishment of what later came to be called the United Nations.

Meanwhile, the situation in the Atlantic heated up for the U.S. Navy. On September 4, 1941, USS *Greer*, a flush deck World War I–era destroyer, was steaming for Iceland alone when a British aircraft radioed a warning

Above: By the fall of 1941, the U.S. Navy had been tasked with escorting Allied convoys through much of the North Atlantic. Such a direct role in the campaign inevitably led to clashes with U-boats, straining American relations with Germany to the breaking point as this undeclared war heated up.

Opposite: The U.S. Navy needed tens of thousands of pilots to man the aircraft just beginning to come off the assembly lines. Here, a class of naval aviation cadets receives last-minute instructions before a training flight in April 1941. Many of these cadets later crewed the patrol bombers that helped beat back the U-boat menace.

to her skipper that a German submarine had been spotted ten miles ahead of his vessel.

Greer's crew members went to general quarters and investigated. They detected *U-652* submerged, but since the Germans made no hostile move, *Greer*'s skipper refused to engage it. The British plane that spotted *U-652* unsuccessfully depth charged the U-boat and then returned to Iceland, leaving *Greer* alone. For three hours, *Greer* remained in contact with the U-boat but did not attack it. After the patrol plane departed, *U-652* fired a torpedo at the old four piper. Her skipper later reported he had attacked one of the fifty destroyers the U.S. Navy turned over the British the previous fall. No such luck.

The Americans spotted the torpedo and dodged it.

Having been fired on, *Greer*'s skipper, Lt. Cmdr. L. H. Frost, launched an attack of his own. After dropping a depth-charge pattern, *Greer* dodged another incoming torpedo. Altogether, the American ship peppered the ocean with nineteen depth charges, but failed to inflict any significant damage to the German submarine. Both warships escaped.

While the lone battle was inconclusive, the consequences were anything but. The attack on *Greer* outraged President Roosevelt, who called it, "an act of piracy." He ordered the armed forces to engage any Axis warships or submarines found in the boundaries of the Western Hemisphere. This became known as the "shoot on sight" order.

THE TYPE VIIC

From 1940 through 1945, the Germans commissioned 568 Type VIIC U-boats. For the majority of the war, these 770-ton submarines formed the backbone of the German navy's silent service. Equipped with 3,000 horsepower worth of diesel engines, the Type VIIC could cut through the swells at almost eighteen knots, faster than many of the early-war Allied escorts. Below the surface, the VIIC relied on 750-horsepower electric motors and could reach almost eight knots submerged, though such speeds would quickly exhaust its battery power.

The VIIC was more a submersible than a true submarine because it was only capable of submerged operations for short intervals. With a range of about eight thousand miles, VIICs were quite effective around the Western Approaches, but needed tanker support to sustain patrols in the New World or South Atlantic.

The heart of these boats was the torpedo rooms. The VIIC came armed with four bow tubes. The stern sported one tube, and the boats carried fourteen torpedoes.

Cramped, smelly, and miserably uncomfortable for their crews, the Type VIIC nevertheless was the most effective ship-killing submarine built during World War II, rivaled only by the American *Gato* class. German crews manning these deadly boats destroyed the majority of the thousands of Allied merchant ships sunk during the Atlantic war.

Above: CV-4, the USS *Ranger*, was the U.S. Navy's first purpose-built aircraft carrier. She served in the Atlantic, supporting the Neutrality Patrols and carried out escort operations in the mid-Atlantic through 1941. She later took part in Operation Torch. Her air group also launched attacks on German shipping in Norway the following year. *Below:* The World War I–era destroyer USS *Du Pont* was a four piper of the *Wickes* class. Prior to Pearl Harbor, she escorted four convoys across the North Atlantic.

Allied warships in Iceland, awaiting their next convoy escort run. The U.S. occupation of that island ensured its safety from any potential German threat in 1941. It also freed up British troops for service in North Africa and helped make Iceland one of the most important bases in the North Atlantic convoy campaign.

Things rapidly spun out of control after the *Greer* incident. On September 14, 1941, the U.S. Navy provided escorts for British convoy HX-150, marking the first time the Americans joined the North Atlantic campaign in a direct role.

HX-150 avoided detection and was not attacked while under American escort. However, about 10 percent of its fifty merchant ships failed to make the crossing. Most of those that didn't reach England suffered mechanical breakdowns. By now, two years of constant fighting and not enough yard time for repairs and maintenance were starting to take their toll on the merchant fleet. On September 24, 1941, the old steamship SS *Nigaristan* suffered a catastrophic fire. Built by a German firm in Bremen in 1913, the ship had been captured in the Indian Ocean by the Allies during World War I. Purchased after the war by the Shahristan Steamship Company, the

vessel had given good service through repeated Atlantic crossings since 1939.

The fire soon blazed out of control and the crew abandoned ship at night in the middle of a massive storm. Driving rain, pitching seas, and gale force winds greeted her crew of sixty-three as they struggled to lower boats and escape their doomed vessel.

The American destroyer USS *Eberle* raced to the rescue. Through the night, the tin can's crew worked furiously to find and haul aboard all the *Nigaristan*'s exhausted survivors. At one point, one of the sailors fell into the heaving swells between his lifeboat and the *Eberle*'s hull. As he floundered in the water, in danger from both drowning and being squashed between his boat and the destroyer, Ensign L. C. Savage swung down on a bowline, grabbed the sailor, and pulled him to safety.

Right: With the men and material to build additional facilities, the Americans went to work transforming Iceland into the lynchpin base for the Allied effort in the North Atlantic. *Below:* Two U.S. airmen investigate the coast of Greenland. In April 1941, the Danish ambassador to the United States signed a treaty with Washington—against his government's directions—that essentially made Greenland a protectorate of the United States.

Anglo-American naval cooperation began long before the United States entered the war. Though it had many rocky moments, these two countries forged the most successful alliance in military history. This photo shows nearly every major player from both navies and governments who helped shape that partnership. Front row, seated: Capt. C. A. Baker, U.S. Navy; Admiral of the Fleet Sir Dudley Pound; J. G. Winant, U.S. ambassador; A. V. Alesander, first lord of the Admiralty; Adm. H. R. Stark, commander of U.S. naval forces in Europe; Prime Minister Winston Churchill; Capt. R. S. Wentworth, U.S. Navy chief of staff; and Capt. H. A. Flanagan, U.S. Navy. Back row: Lt. Cmdr. H. R. Hardy; Rear Adm. A. L. St. George Lyster, fifth sea lord; Lord Bruntisfield; Col. Sir Eric Crankshawe; Vice Adm. Sir W. J. Whitworth; Second Sea Lord Cmdr. Thompson; Vice Adm. Sir H. A. Fraser, third sea lord; Vice Adm. Ernest King, U. S. Navy; Vice Adm. Sir J. R. Cunningham, fourth sea lord; Rear Adm. H. B. Rawlings; Adm. Sir Percy Noble; Rear Adm. R. H. McGrigor; Capt. T. A. Selberg; Rear Adm. A. J. Power; Sir Geoffrey Blake; Cmdr. E. N. Litoh; Sir J. S. Barnes; Capt. R. A. Pilkington, civil lord; Rear Adm. A. M. Peters, and Lt. A. J. Vessey, U.S. Navy.

All sixty-three men were rescued. The incident impressed the Royal Navy and helped set the stage for the mutual respect and remarkable cooperation that grew between the U.S. Navy and the Royal Navy in the years to come.

A month later, convoy SC-48's fifty merchant ships departed the New World for a slow-motion churn across the Atlantic's wild seas. Storms and mechanical failures caused eleven ships to fall out of formation. Even at seven knots, the thirty-nine ships left in the convoy's nine columns could barely keep station.

Four hundred miles south of Iceland, SC-48 stumbled into a wolf pack. The wolves picked off three ships in one night. The convoy called for help, and an escort force from Iceland sortied to the rescue. This included five American destroyers, a Free French corvette, and the HMS *Broadwater*, one of the fifty World War–I flush deck tin cans given to the Royal Navy during the Destroyers for Bases deal.

The reinforcements arrived just before sunset on October 16. That night, five subs attacked again. Air

(continued on page 160)

Above: British warships steam past the American battleship USS *Mississippi* at Hvalfjord, Iceland, in October 1941. She spent the fall of 1941 protecting convoys in the North Atlantic. *Opposite top: Prinz Eugen* survived its sortie with *Bismarck* to become an enduring thorn in the Allies' side after it deployed to Norway. There, the Allies feared it could either break out for another raiding mission into the Atlantic or conduct surface attacks on the Arctic convoys bound for Russia. *Opposite bottom:* The Bethlehem shipyard in Baltimore, Maryland, seen in October 1941. America's industrial power to construct a two-ocean navy, plus supply the Allies with millions of tons of merchant shipping, represented one of the greatest feats in history.

Above: The *Tribal*-class destroyer, HMS *Matabele* seen in Hvalfjord Harbor in the fall of 1941. The *Matabele* was sunk by *U-454* in January 1942 while escorting Arctic convoy PQ-8. *Opposite:* Following the sinking of the USS *Reuben James*, the U.S. Navy named a brand-new destroyer escort in her honor. Launched in February 1943 as DE-153, the new *Reuben James* served through the final two years of the war escorting convoys in the Atlantic and Mediterranean.

(continued from page 157)
cover detected four of them and forced them to dive. The fifth, Kapitänleutnant Karl Thurmann's *U-553*, cagily used rain squalls and the heavy seas to sneak past the destroyer USS *Plunkett* to launch a spread of torpedoes. One struck HMS *Gladiolus*, a *Flower*-class corvette, and detonated the ship's magazine. The little vessel was blown apart with the loss of her entire crew. Destroyer USS *Kearney* then forced Thurmann to dive, but his attack set the stage for the rest of a long and dreadful night.

Ninety minutes after *U-553* attacked, *U-558* torpedoed three merchant ships. Heinz-Otto Schultze's *U-432* waded into the fray next, sinking three ships in quick succession. The inexperienced escort force fired star shells, dropped depth charges randomly, and sped around the convoy's flanks in a fruitless search for the attacking submarines. In the rollercoaster seas, merchant ships exploded and burned. Men tumbled into the swells and scrabbled onto whatever floating wreckage they could find.

At one point, destroyer USS *Kearney* steamed past a burning tanker. Backlit by its hellish red-orange glow, the American ship was spotted by *U-568*, whose skipper sent a torpedo her way. The eel slammed into *Kearney* amidships, killing eleven U.S. Navy sailors. These eleven were the first American servicemen to be killed in combat during World War II. *Kearney* limped to Iceland, out of the fight. Not long after she departed, *U-101* torpedoed and sank HMS *Broadwater*.

That fall, American destroyers covered British convoys between Newfoundland and Iceland. The U.S. Navy vessels assigned to this duty were stationed out of Iceland, which had by now become a vital component to the Allied effort in the Atlantic.

USS *Reuben James* was one of those venerable four pipers pressed into convoy escort duty. Commissioned in 1920, she carried a quartet of 4-inch guns, four triple-torpedo tube mounts, and twin depth-charge racks on her stern. She had served with both the Atlantic and Pacific Fleets during the interwar years, and had taken part in relief operations in the Mediterranean and

Above: Placentia Bay, Newfoundland. In the fall of 1941, there were little facilities there, and the American PBY and PBM flying boats operating out of the bay relied on seaplane tenders for resupply. *Below:* The German invasion of Russia altered the naval war in the Atlantic. Winston Churchill promised aid to Stalin. To make good on this promise, the Royal Navy had to strip ships from the Atlantic and Mediterranean to escort the Arctic convoys. *Opposite:* An *Omaha*-class light cruiser serving with the U.S. Navy's South Atlantic Patrol.

served with the blockade force off the Nicaraguan coast during the 1920s. A veteran of the Neutrality Patrols, by the fall of 1941 she was based out of Iceland and had already escorted convoy ON-20 at the start of October. On the twenty-fourth of the month, she joined inbound convoy HX-156 along with four other destroyers under Cmdr. R. E. Web.

The crossing was uneventful until October 30, when some six hundred miles west of Ireland, HX-156 attracted the attention of Erich Topp's *U-552*, a Type VIIC U-boat that had joined the fleet the previous December. By October 1941, Topp had completed four harrowing war patrols in the boat, which the rest of the Kriegsmarine called *Der Rote Teufel* (The Red Devil) as a result of the insignia painted on *U-552*'s conning tower.

On October 30, 1941, Topp was maneuvering on HX-156 when *Reuben James* presented herself as a target. The Hanoverian fired two torpedoes, one of which hit *Reuben James* in the bow. Her forward magazine exploded and blew most of the ship apart. Only a chunk of the stern survived the blast to stay afloat for a few more minutes. No officers survived, and only 45 men of the 159 aboard were rescued. One survivor subsequently died of his wounds.

The sinking of *Reuben James* destroyed the last vestiges of American neutrality. After the Germans refused to apologize for the attack, Congress repealed the Neutrality Acts. American vessels could legally steam to England now. The United States also began arming its merchant fleet.

After a lull in the late spring and summer, U-boat attacks spiked in the fall. In September, fifty-six ships representing 209,835 tons were lost to German submarines. October saw forty-five more go down. As distressing as this was to the British, the Kriegsmarine had not been able to duplicate their devastating successes of late 1940—even with a significantly larger U-boat force.

Now that the U.S. Navy had joined the fight, the German submariners faced a new set of challenges. But Doenitz had one more card to play before the Americans could conquer their learning curve. The result would be the last great merchant ship slaughter of the Atlantic war.

CHAPTER NINE

THE DAY TOURISM DIED

The Japanese attack on Pearl Harbor changed the complexion of the Battle of the Atlantic. Four days after the surprise attack on the Pacific Fleet, Hitler and Mussolini declared war on the United States. Germany, already stretched thin by the invasion of Russia, now faced an enemy power whose industrial output would out soon outmatch anything ever seen in history.

For the U-boat force, already fighting an increasingly formidable foe in the Royal Navy, the declaration of war meant two things. First, it gave Adm. Karl Doenitz an opportunity to hit American shipping lanes along the Eastern Seaboard and the Caribbean, which were largely undefended and unconvoyed. It would take time for the United States to organize an effective defense. Until it did, Doenitz planned to do as much damage as possible.

Second, and more important in the long run, the German declaration of war meant that the U-boat force would have to fight against what would soon be the largest navy on the planet. Though less experienced than the British, the U.S. Navy would soon include the most reliable and well-armed ASW vessels on the planet. With the U.S. Navy in the fight, Doenitz's chance to achieve victory in the Atlantic faded.

On December 12, 1941, Doenitz met with Admiral Raeder to discuss Operation Paukenschlag—a.k.a. Operation Drumroll—the plan to deploy U-boats to U.S. coastal waters.

Doenitz told Raeder he needed a month to get his boats in place, and they faced daunting challenges just in getting there. The distance to U.S. shores was so vast that the Type VII crews would need to cram every nook and cranny aboard their boats with extra fuel. The men responded admirably. Some crews went so far as to fill reserve water tanks with diesel. Others stashed cans of fuel away in bunks and food lockers, and between the engines themselves. The already miserably cramped conditions in these tiny submersibles became nearly intolerable with these field expedients. But they worked. The boats eventually made it to America.

Doenitz really wanted to deploy his larger Type IX boats to the America operation, but Raeder denied him their use—at least at first. The U-boat force had suffered heavy losses over the past year, and the demands of the Mediterranean theater, along with commitments in the far north around Norway, meant few boats were available for Operation Drumroll. Raeder initially released

Opposite: A convoy under attack by *U-130*. In the opening weeks of the war, the U.S. Navy refused to establish a convoy system for the coastal merchant shipping lanes, which set the stage for a national catastrophe.

FLORIDA IN THE U-BOAT WAR

When Adm. Karl Doenitz's wolves reached the American East Coast during Operation Drumroll, the boats soon began hunting targets off the Florida coast. Backlit by the coastal communities and their refusal to blackout their towns, merchant ships running off shore made for easy pickings for the veteran U-boat crews. Twenty-four ships went down off the Florida coastline, many of which exploded and sank in full view of horrified civilians watching from beaches. Bodies of merchant seamen, debris, and slicks of oil from lost tankers soon coated those beaches and drove the tourists away.

In one incident, U-boat ace Reinhard Hardegen caught the U.S. tanker SS *Gulf America* just four miles off the beaches of Jacksonville, Florida, on the night of April 11, 1942. Unarmed and unescorted, the crew could only await their fate as they watched Hardegen's surfaced boat steam into range. The German ace maneuvered between his target and the coast before opening fire with his deck gun. This way, he negated any chance a long shot would kill civilians on the coast.

Years later, the famous U-boat skipper visited Jacksonville to receive a warm welcome for his rare act of wartime chivalry.

only five Type VIICs and one longer-ranged IXB. On January 2, 1942, however, the grand admiral relented and gave Doenitz seven Type IXs for the new offensive.

Thirteen boats for the Eastern Seaboard did not seem like much, but it represented the major deployment for the U-boat force in early 1942. The mission was carried out by denuding the North Atlantic of submarines. From January to April 1942, few of the British-bound convoys came under attack, but that was the only good news for the Allies.

Doenitz had a total of ninety-one operational boats, twenty-three of which were in the Mediterranean, while four others were stationed off Norway to intercept the Allied supply runs to and from Russia. Of the remaining fifty-eight, about half were in dockyards waiting for upgrades, overhauls, or repairs. That left twenty-two boats for the Atlantic, half of which would be in transit to assigned hunting grounds at any given time. Two years into the fighting and the Germans had yet to be able to deploy a significantly larger U-boat presence in the most critical theater of the war.

On January 12, 1942, the Type IX boat *U-123* opened Operation Drumroll with an attack some three hundred miles off the coast of Cape Cod, Massachusetts.

Commanded by ace Reinhard Hardegen, *U-123* had sunk twenty-two ships over the course of numerous Atlantic patrols since joining the fleet in the spring of 1940.

Hardegen's first attack of the new campaign netted SS *Cyclops*, a British cargo ship of nine thousand tons. She went down with eighty-seven men.

The attack signaled the onset of a shipping slaughter unmatched in World War II. The U.S. Navy refused to adopt a convoy system due to a shortage of escorts and a desire to use the available ASW assets on offensive sweeps. Admiral Ernest King, recently appointed as chief of naval operations, believed that a convoy with light or no escort was more vulnerable than if the ships sailed independently. Imbued with an offensive spirit, he wanted to take the fight to the U-boats.

These were bankrupt ideas, proven false both at the end of World War I and in the early days of World War II. The U.S. Navy failed to learn those lessons, much to the frustration of the British.

The merchant marine paid the price for this mistaken strategy. When the German boats reached their coastal hunting grounds, their skippers—jaded from months of pitched, desperate battles against the able Royal Navy—discovered a nation's maritime fleet operating under

A U.S. Navy Grumman Duck light utility aircraft. Ducks served in small numbers throughout the navy's commands along the Eastern Seaboard and were used on several occasions to rescue survivors of U-boat attacks.

Above: In January 1942, the Kriegsmarine unleashed a new offensive along America's lightly defended coastal shipping in what became known as Operation Drumroll. *Below:* The Chance-Vought OS2U Kingfisher replaced the SOC Seagull as the U.S. Navy's standard shipboard scout floatplane. During the desperate first weeks of the war, the Kingfishers were pressed into service on antisubmarine patrols along the East Coast.

While the Germans pressed their coastal attacks, most of Doenitz's boats pulled out of the North Atlantic. Few convoys between Canada and Great Britain were attacked during Operation Drumroll, a small consolation to the Allies, who were reeling under the impact of the merchant shipping slaughter being carried out just off America's shores.

peacetime conditions. The merchant crews followed no light or smoke discipline. They followed no zigzag pattern to throw off torpedo attacks. Most of the ships had not yet been fitted with weaponry to ward off surface attacks, and the threat of air attack was slight. With the sea lanes choked with easy targets, the few U-boats deployed to the area ran riot.

As in the North Atlantic, the U-boats stalked their prey at night. The skippers found choice spots where they would hunker down during the day. Once the sun set, the boats would surface and glide through the calm seas in search of victims. Their hunting was materially aided by the American coastal communities, such as Atlantic City and Miami, whose city fathers refused

to follow basic blackout procedures out of fear that it would kill off the tourist trade.

The lights silhouetted the Allied ships plying the nearby waters. Backlit, their outlines perfectly visible to the U-boats, these ships had no chance. Dozens went down right offshore from New Jersey down to Florida. The beaches—the prime tourist attraction for most of these coastal communities—were fouled with oil, debris, and the bodies of the merchant seamen the city lights helped kill.

The carnage was made worse in February when the German navy changed its Enigma system and incorporated a fourth rotor in its machines. This effectively blinded Bletchley Park and the British code

In early 1942, the defenses along the North American coast were still underdeveloped and primitive. In Argentia, Newfoundland, the USS *Richard Peck* served as a temporary floating barracks for the sub-hunting units based there.

breakers for the better part of the year—at a time that was utterly crucial to the Allied cause.

The situation became a national catastrophe—and disgrace. The British looked on in horror as two years of hard-fought experience was ignored by their new allies. Ships that the Royal Navy spent considerable effort getting across the Atlantic were taken out in North American waters. It was fertile ground for the U-boats. Over fifty ships a day entered New York from the St. Lawrence River alone. Kapitänleutnant Hardegen and *U-123* had a typical first cruise during Drumroll's opening weeks. After sinking *Cyclops* on January 12, 1942, Hardegen took his boat within sight of Long Island two nights later to sink the 9,577-ton Panamanian-registered tanker SS *Norness*. On the fifteenthth, while off New York, an American aircraft attacked Hardegen's boat on the surface. The big Type IX plunged beneath the waves in a crash dive that spared it serious damage.

Off Cape Hatteras four nights later, Hardegen rampaged through the coastal traffic, sinking five ships

totaling more than 19,000 tons. With its tubes empty and one engine offline as a result of mechanical failure, *U-123* was spotted by a Norwegian whaling ship, the *Kosmos II*. Her skipper, Master Einar Gleditsch, cranked his big vessel up to seventeen knots and charged Hardegen's Type IX.

The German boat turned and fled, but the Norwegians slowly gained. With no time to dive, Hardegen faced the unsavory prospect of being run down by an unarmed whaling ship. As the distance closed to seventy-five meters, *U-123*'s engineers repaired their ailing engine and got it restarted. They gave Hardegen eighteen knots—just enough to effect a slow-motion escape.

Hardegen sank two more ships before heading back to Lorient, returning on February 9, 1942. His crew had been at sea for forty-nine days. A short refit and shore leave later, the boat departed for American waters again on March 2. By then, the massacre was in full swing, aided by B-Dienst's intercepts of Anglo-American-Canadian signal traffic.

Above: A U.S. Navy warship drops a depth charge on a sound contact. American antisubmarine warcraft defenses along the Eastern Seaboard, Caribbean, and Gulf of Mexico were so minimal that the German U-boats operated with impunity. Some surfaced and scored kills in harbors; others sank targets within sight of American beachcombers relaxing on shore. *Below:* The SS *Tiger* heads for the bottom during Operation Drumroll.

Above: The sinking of the SS *Robert Tuttle* in June 1942. Caught off Cape Henry, she was one of the scores of tankers sunk during the U-boat onslaught in the New World. *Below:* The SS *Dixie Arrow* was another tanker lost. This one went down off Cape Hatteras at the end of March 1942.

Survivors of a U-boat attack are spotted by an aerial patrol somewhere off the U.S. coast.

In January, Doenitz's new campaign sank forty-eight ships, totaling 276,795 tons. In February, the Germans extended their offensive into the Caribbean. Thirty-one ships were sunk off America's shores, while another thirty-three went down in the Caribbean. Combined with sinkings elsewhere by U-boats in the Northern Hemisphere, the Allies lost seventy-three ships and 429,891 tons of shipping that month.

March proved to be a complete disaster. As the U-boats continued to run amok off the United States, the Japanese successes in the Pacific, and the bloody fighting in the Mediterranean Sea, the Allies lost a grand total of 273 ships. That removed 834,164 tons of sealift capability from the cause.

Doenitz's strategy to strangle England depended on destroying merchant ships faster than they could be replaced. In 1942, the German naval staff calculated that just to keep pace with estimated Allied new construction,

the U-boat crews needed to sink a minimum of 700,000 tons a month. The actual number was 590,000.

The final weeks of 1941 had seen a decline in sinkings, but the year's total had been brutal for the British, who lost almost 2.6 million tons to all causes. Britain was unable to keep pace with the losses. Lend-Lease and the U.S. entry into the war saved the day.

Through 1942, the British and Canadians built 1.5 million tons of dry goods cargo ships. The United States planned to complete seven million, but actually produced nine. The massive construction program was made possible by the quality of the American shipyards and the adoption of mass production techniques. Where it took British yards months to produce a vessel, the United States became so adept at it that one company could build and launch a Liberty Ship in just twenty-four hours. The United States produced more than 2,800

(continued on page 176)

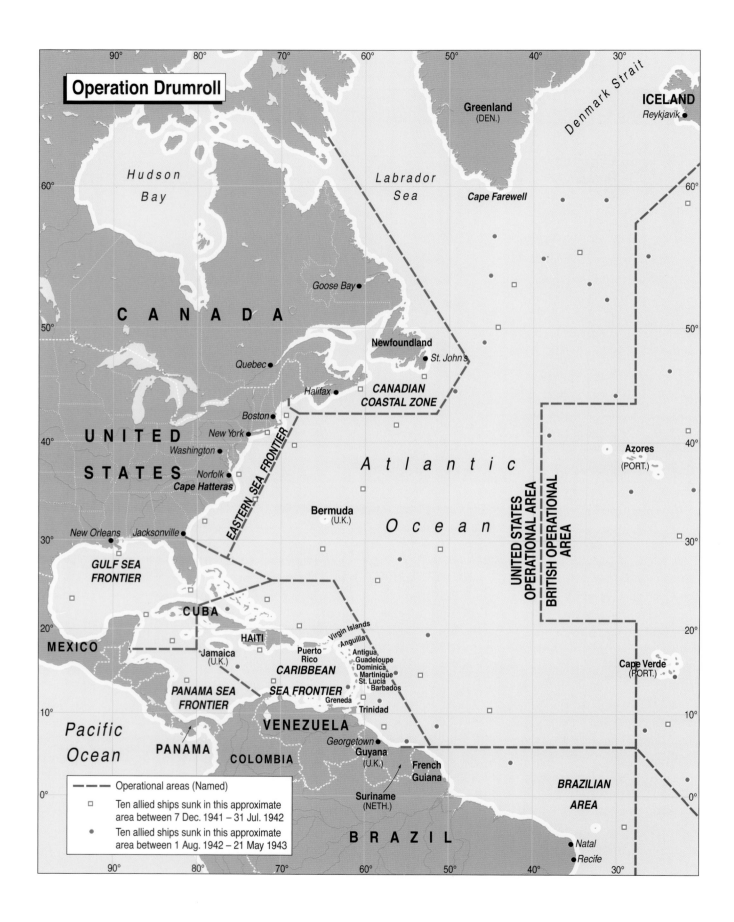

Operation Drumroll

Legend:

— — — Operational areas (Named)

□ Ten allied ships sunk in this approximate area between 7 Dec. 1941 – 31 Jul. 1942

● Ten allied ships sunk in this approximate area between 1 Aug. 1942 – 21 May 1943

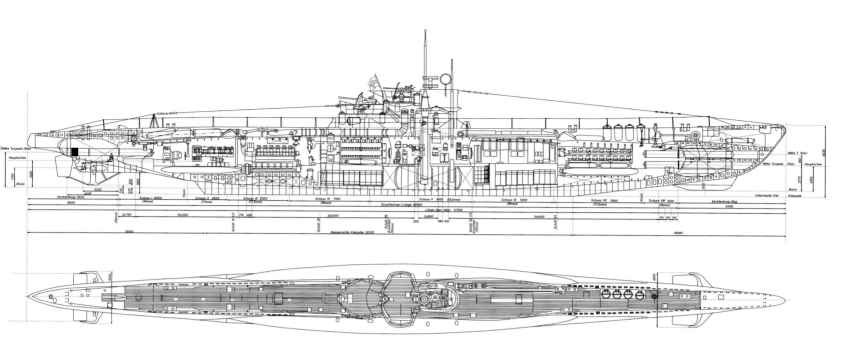

Above: Over five hundred Type VIIC U-boats were commissioned between 1940 and 1945, the most numerous in the German navy. The Type VIIC *U-96* was the inspiration for the 1973 novel *Das Boot*, which was made into a film of the same name in 1981. *The-Blueprints.com Below:* The large Type IXC had additional fuel storage capacity even beyond previous Type IXs. The Type IXC *U-505* was captured by the U.S. Navy in June 1944 and is currently on display at Chicago's Museum of Science and Industry. *The-Blueprints.com*

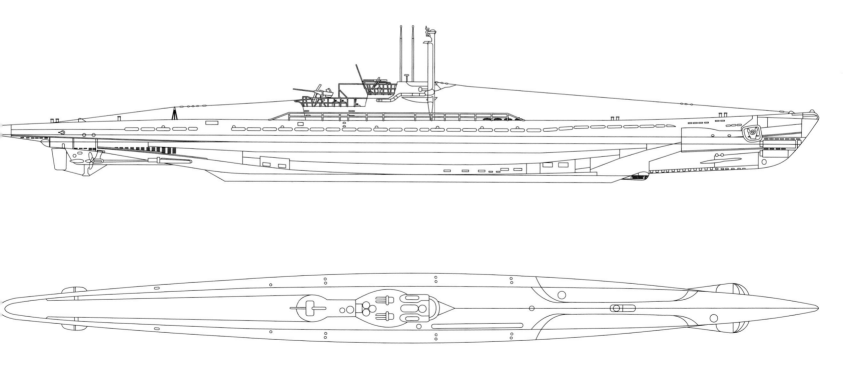

Above: It wasn't until the spring of 1942 that a convoy system was established along the East Coast. As the defenses gradually stiffened, Doenitz shifted the focus of his operations to the Caribbean and the Gulf of Mexico. *Opposite:* A U-boat crew's view of the fiery end to a vital Allied tanker.

(continued from page 173)
of these crucial vessels—almost thirty million tons of cargo vessels alone. The U-boat crews simply could not sink them fast enough. It is no exaggeration to say that the venerable Liberty Ship became one of the cornerstones to the Allied victory.

The same efficiency and industrial might was put behind the escort construction effort. By the end of 1941, almost three hundred escorts were being built in the United States. In April 1942, a "sixty escorts in sixty days" campaign began, and by May 4, sixty-seven had been finished.

As more ships joined the fleet, the U.S. Navy needed capable, well-trained men to take them into the fight. In March 1942, a dedicated antisubmarine warfare school was established in Miami. Over the next two years, 10,396 officers and 37,574 enlisted men graduated from

it. In the months to come, they would join the fight in the Atlantic in an ever-increasing torrent.

While the yards cranked out new vessels, the American defenses along the Eastern Sea Frontier slowly began to stiffen. Initially, the British pitched in by loaning the U.S. Navy some of its escorts. That helped, but the way the available assets were employed needed to change. So far, not a single U-boat had been sunk off the East Coast, and the offensive sweeps effectively neutralized what escorts the navy possessed.

It took an appalling five months of slaughter before the U.S. Navy's senior leadership threw in the towel on their long-discredited strategy. In mid-May, the coastal traffic was finally organized into convoys. Shortly afterward, Admiral King confessed that the offensive sweeps accomplished nothing and ordered them halted. What antisubmarine warfare capabilities the surface fleet in

Above: Loading locomotives aboard a cargo vessel for the transatlantic crossing. The United States not only became the "Arsenal of Democracy," but it provided its industrial might to help sustain the transportation system in Europe. Locomotives became a particularly high priority cargo after D-Day when the Allies needed to rebuild France's ruined rail system. *Below:* A convoy under attack by a submerged U-boat. Such daylight attacks were not terribly common until later in 1942.

the Atlantic possessed would now be dedicated to covering the convoys—at least for the next several months.

The civilians on the East Coast gradually awoke to the realities of the war. After four months of bodies, debris, and fuel oil washing up on their beaches, the cities finally adhered to a general blackout starting on April 18. No longer would concern for tourism make hunting even easier for the Germans.

At the same time, the available ASW aircraft steadily grew. At the start of the war, the U.S. Navy had only four U-boat hunting squadrons to cover the Atlantic from Maine to Jacksonville, Florida. At the end of March, the Eastern Sea Frontier command included eighteen airfields, eighty-three U.S. Navy aircraft, four blimps, and eighty-four USAAF aircraft.

Still, less than two hundred aircraft to protect seven thousand miles worth of sea lanes was a paltry number. Reinforcements flowed in, and by mid-summer 1942, the Eastern Sea Frontier boasted twenty-six airfields and more than three hundred U.S. Navy and U.S. Army Air Force aircraft, plus seven blimps.

As all this was being organized, the U.S. Navy scored its first U-boat kill of the war. On March 15, 1942, a VP-82 Lockheed Hudson based out of Argentina discovered and sank *U-503* off the coast of Newfoundland

The surface navy soon bagged its first boat as well. On the night of April 13–14, 1942, USS *Roper* discovered *U-85* on the surface not far from the Cape Bodie Lighthouse off North Carolina. With less than a hundred feet of water under the *U-85*'s hull, her crew could not escape by crash-diving. A running nighttime gun battle broke out between the old four-piper and the year-old Type VIIB boat near Cape Hatteras. The *Roper*'s crew managed to score a hit with one of the ship's 3-inch guns that penetrated *U-85*'s pressure hull. The German crew promptly abandoned their boat. As their boat sank, *Roper* delivered a final depth charge attack. About half *U-85*'s crew had made it into the water when eleven depth charges exploded beneath them. Not a man survived.

Roper's skipper, fearing a second U-boat might be in the area, waited until daylight to try to rescue *U-85*'s crew. When they returned that morning, the Americans found twenty-nine dead submariners floating in their

Johann Mohr, skipper of *U-124*, was one of the most successful U-boat aces during Operation Drumroll. He and his crew sank twenty-nine ships, totaling 135,067 tons, before meeting their end off Gibraltar in April 1943.

life jackets. Their bodies were collected, then later buried with full military honors during a nocturnal ceremony in Hampton National Cemetery. Curiously, some of the crew carried American currency and were dressed in civilian clothes.

At least one German account of *U-85*'s sinking has accused the United States of war crimes for failing to rescue the crew in a timely manner.

A month later, on May 9, 1942, the coast guard sank its first U-boat. The Type VIIC boat, *U-352*, was on its

One of the notorious "Yippie Boats"—tiny, ad hoc escorts that held the line until U.S. shipyards could start cranking out better ASW warships.

second patrol with a skipper who one crewmember later claimed was obsessed with winning the Knight's Cross. At the time, this required destroying a hundred thousand tons of shipping, but *U-352* had yet to sink a ship. As the patrol wore on, Korvettenkapitän Hellmut Rathke grew increasingly reckless. That led him into shallow waters off Cape Hatteras, where *U-352* was detected by the coast guard cutter *Icarus*. The boat tried to dive to avoid the American vessel, but the cutter's crew hammered *U-352* with depth charges. Thirty-three men, including the boat's glory-hunting captain, survived the attack. Fifteen were lost when *U-532* sank.

By May 1942, as American defenses stiffened along the East Coast, Doenitz shifted the emphasis of Drumroll to the Caribbean and the Gulf of Mexico. The arrival of brand-new "milch cow" tanker submarines, designated Type XIVs, ensured that the other subs could operate

deep into both the Caribbean and the Gulf. The first milch cow on station was *U-459*, and at 1,700 tons, it carried enough provisions and fuel to keep twelve Type VIICs supplied for an extra month at sea.

Some five hundred miles off Bemuda, *U-459* serviced its first customer, *U-108*. Within a week and a half, this first milch cow had fueled a dozen Type VIIs and two Type IXs. Later joined by another milch cow, *U-460*, plus *U-116* (a Type X minelayer), these logistic support submarines sustained the offensives in the Caribbean and Gulf of Mexico.

In May and June, five Italian boats joined the Type IXs and VIIs. With few escorts and even fewer aircraft in the area, the Axis subs once again went on a frenzy of destruction. In May, the Italians sank three ships for 18,333 tons, while the Germans destroyed twenty-six in the Gulf of Mexico and another forty-eight in

Above: An Allied cargo ship limps for home after taking a torpedo hit. *Below:* Two small Allied escorts. Such ships were so slow that U-boats could outrun them on the surface. They carried light armament, a few depth charges, and ASDIC, making them only marginally effective.

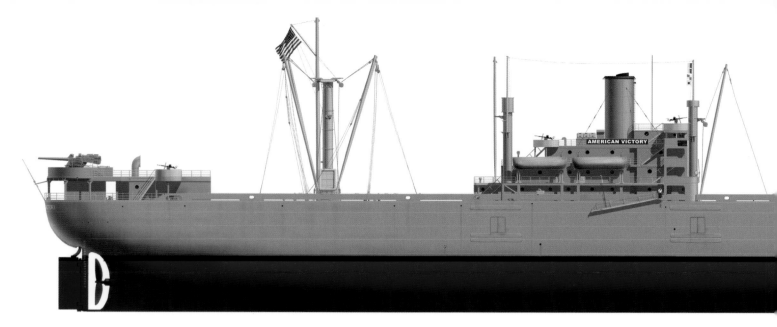

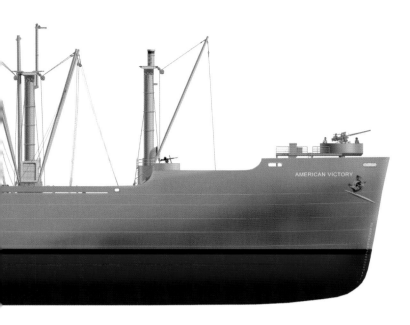

Left: SS *American Victory* is a *Victory*-class cargo ship, which was modeled on the *Liberty* ships, but larger and with design improvements that increased speed. The ship served in the Pacific from June 20, 1945, until the end of the war. The *American Victory* is currently a museum ship in Tampa, Florida. *Chris Sheppard*

Bottom: The SS *Henry Sinclair Jr.* burns furiously after taking a torpedo hit from *U-203* off the North Carolina coast on April 11, 1942.

the Caribbean. The U-boat skippers grew increasingly brazen as they encountered feeble opposition. Ace Albrecht Achilles conned his new Type IXC boat, *U-161*, into Castries Harbor, St. Lucia, on the surface one night. There he found a cornucopia of shipping sitting at anchor. He torpedoed a passenger ship and a freighter, then made off in the night with his running lights blazing.

These were long patrols for the Germans, who had been averaging thirty to sixty days out at sea up until Drumroll. Achilles and his crew returned to Lorient after a hundred days in the tropics. The addition of the Type XIV milch cows made such extended patrols a reality and their value to Drumroll and the U-boat arm's strategic reach was crucial to the next year of the war in the Atlantic.

By the end of May, total worldwide losses for the month came to 705,050 tons and 151 ships. At the same time, both the British and American navies had been taking a beating in the Pacific. Most of the American Asiatic fleet was destroyed in the Philippines or the Dutch East Indies. Then came the Battle of the Coral Sea and the loss of the carrier USS *Lexington*. The Royal Navy suffered proportionately greater losses. In December 1941, the Japanese sank the battle cruiser HMS *Repulse* and *Prince of Wales*. The defeat at Singapore cost the British a number of destroyers as well. In the Mediterranean, the Axis air-sea operations against the British fleets sustaining the island fortress of Malta continued to inflict heavy casualties. The carrier *Ark Royal* was torpedoed and sunk by a U-boat. The battleship *Barham* was lost, and Italian frogmen severely damaged the battlewagons *Queen Elizabeth* and *Valiant* in Alexandria harbor. Two cruisers and a destroyer were also neutralized.

Above: The tanker SS *Persephone* sinks off the New Jersey coast on May 25, 1942. She was sunk by torpedo attack by *U-593. Left:* The end of the Latvian cargo ship *Ciltavaria*. Her back broken by a torpedo hit, she went down off the U.S. coast in January 1942, one of Drumroll's first victims.

In June, the crisis reached its peak. One hundred seventy-three ships went down, representing the highest monthly tonnage total of the war—834,196. One hundred forty-four of those vessels were lost to submarines, and of that, 60 percent met their doom in the Gulf of Mexico and Caribbean.

In light of the massive fleet losses, set against the backdrop of Drumroll's gruesome toll, it looked to many Allied leaders that their cause was in serious jeopardy. At the height of the crisis, the chief of the U.S. Army, Gen. George Marshall, wrote to Adm. Ernest King an extraordinary letter that read, in part: "The losses by submarines off our Atlantic seaboard and in the Caribbean now threaten our entire war effort."

Marshall went on to note that 22 percent of the bauxite fleet available to the Allies had been sunk since January, 20 percent of Puerto Rico's merchant ships had been sunk, and the attrition rate of tankers stood at 3.5 percent a month.

Marshall had hit on a vital point. From January to June 1942, the U.S. lost seventy-three tankers in the Atlantic and coastal waters. The British lost another sixty-eight. So many had gone down that the United States halted all tanker movement along the coastal lanes until the convoy system could be established to

American coastal communities refused to extinguish their lights at night for fear of driving tourists away. Without blackout conditions, ships sailing along the coast were backlit by these cities, making them easy targets for waiting U-boats. The beaches along the American East Coast were soon covered with corpses, oil slicks, and debris, which killed off the tourist trade anyway.

An American PBY flying boat follows an oil slick in search of survivors following a U-boat attack. With only a handful of submarines, Doenitz's men sank 350 merchant ships—over 2.5 million tons—in what became the worst shipping slaughter of the war. The Germans lost eight submarines.

better protect them. These losses forced the British to ration gas even more stringently.

But the "Second Happy Time," as Drumroll came to be known by the U-boat crews, had reached its end. The level of losses forced the Americans to deploy even greater resources to counter the threat. The U.S. Navy and U.S. Coast Guard destroyed more German U-boats that summer, and Doenitz realized the days of easy pickings were over. He called a halt to the operation. By early September, the U-boats returned in force to the North Atlantic, and once again the wolf packs waded into the England-bound convoys.

Drumroll had been a resounding victory for the German navy. From January to June 1942, the Axis sank almost a thousand Allied ships. Nearly six hundred

of those went down at the hands of German, Italian, and Japanese submarines. Drumroll destroyed about four hundred of those.

Five thousand Allied sailors died in the Gulf, the Caribbean, and off the Eastern Seaboard during that period. In fact, a quarter of all the merchant ships destroyed during World War II went down during Drumroll. And yet, for all the destruction inflicted, Doenitz could not sustain the damage long enough to cripple the Allies' sealift capacity. There were simply too many Liberty ships on the slips in American yards.

Instead of being the straw that broke the back of the Anglo-American war effort, Drumroll became the U-boat's last hurrah.

CHAPTER TEN

LIFE ON THE WAVES

For every hardship and misery experienced by the U-boat men, the Allied merchant seamen could match or exceed it. These civilians, who for decades were not even considered veterans, played the most vital role for the Allied cause during World War II. Without their endurance and courage, England would have succumbed before the United States could enter the war. Even after Pearl Harbor, the war still could have been lost if the merchant marine had not given its last full measure.

Going to sea in ancient, rusting freighters, thrown into service as a result of the desperate shipping shortage, took no small amount of guts. Some ships could barely make five knots and handled poorly in heavy seas. Weather was a constant enemy. In winter, they faced icebergs that would tear open their thin hulls and pitching swells so severe that they sometimes crippled ships. As the crisis grew, the men received little rest, and their vessels were forced to go without basic overhauls. Exhaustion led to mistakes at crucial times, while the lack of maintenance often caused engine breakdowns in the middle of the Atlantic where U-boats waited for the easy kill of stragglers.

When they did encounter U-boats, fate was cruel to these men. Aboard tankers, few survived when their cargos caught fire. They burned to death in the flames. In the cargo ships, the crews faced equally grim fates. Ships heavily laden with steel or iron ore rode badly in the water, and when struck by torpedoes they sank in seconds with few survivors. Those unlucky to draw ammunition as their cargo faced the proposition of blowing up if hit. When an ammunition ship did explode, the blast would rain debris on other ships for miles around.

At least that was a quick end. Countless times, merchant seamen escaped their doomed vessels only to die of exposure as they floated in lifeboats. Occasionally, those men who did reach lifeboats were machine gunned by the U-boat that sank their vessel, though this happened far less frequently than has been alleged over the years by Allied sources. In 1941, dedicated rescue ships were assigned to each convoy. Doenitz quietly made these ships targets.

Altogether, about eighty thousand merchant mariners died during the war. They suffered a higher loss rate than even the U.S. Marine Corps. For all their sacrifice, both Britain and the United States resisted giving veteran's benefits to these men who paved the way to victory in World War II. The photos in the following pages offer a glimpse of what life was like for these unheralded heroes.

Opposite: Merchant seamen receive vaccines prior to an Atlantic crossing.

Doenitz's tonnage war was a campaign of numbers and industrial capacity. Lost in that Teutonic equation was the human toll such a bloody war of attrition inflicted.

Left: Old man's eyes characterized even the youngest merchant seamen who dared the odds and served on the Atlantic runs. Pictured here is Richard Brown, a British merchant mariner, a North Atlantic veteran at age twenty-one. *Below:* American merchant mariners await their next assignments at the port of New York City.

Above: After the United States entered the war, New York City became a central hub of convoy activity for the Atlantic crossings. This photo shows the port's nerve center and the map upon which every vessel in the harbor was tracked. *Right:* The workhorse of the Atlantic war became the venerable Liberty ship—mass-produced cargo vessels that saw service in vast numbers. Sometimes built in a matter of days, they poured into the Atlantic in numbers Doenitz's wolves could not possibly counter. This one carries a deck load of North American P-51 Mustangs for the U.S. Army Air Force units in England.

Right: Recognition of the merchant marine's contribution to the war effort was infrequent at best. This was one of the rare occasions when President Roosevelt decorated a merchant mariner in a wartime White House ceremony. Even seventy years later, the role the merchant marine played in the final Allied victory has received scant attention. *Below:* The merchant marine served as the logistical muscle for the Allied cause. Every truck, tank, jeep, rifle, and artillery shell used by the United States during the war was carried by the merchant marine across hostile seas to the distant battlefields.

Above: SS *Martaban* at sea in 1944. Built in 1934, she survived the war, though she had two very close brushes with Davy Jones's locker in the course of her many trips across the Indian Ocean and Atlantic. *Below:* A typical Liberty ship, seen at sea in 1944. Unlike the cargo vessels of 1939 to 1941, these vessels were well-armed with 3-inch and 5-inch guns, plus a suite of 40mm and 20mm antiaircraft guns.

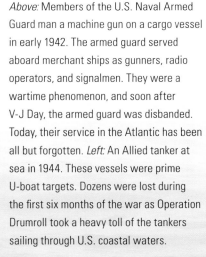

Above: Members of the U.S. Naval Armed Guard man a machine gun on a cargo vessel in early 1942. The armed guard served aboard merchant ships as gunners, radio operators, and signalmen. They were a wartime phenomenon, and soon after V-J Day, the armed guard was disbanded. Today, their service in the Atlantic has been all but forgotten. *Left:* An Allied tanker at sea in 1944. These vessels were prime U-boat targets. Dozens were lost during the first six months of the war as Operation Drumroll took a heavy toll of the tankers sailing through U.S. coastal waters.

Above: Members of the U.S. Naval Armed Guard arrive in a New York hotel prior to assignment to their new commands. *Below:* Merchant mariners learned to load and fire a 5-inch gun, freshly mounted on their cargo ship in 1942. Until late 1941, U.S. law prevented the American merchant navy from arming its vessels. That changed in the wake of the *Reuben James* loss.

Left: Naval armed guard personnel stand watch aboard a freshly armed cargo vessel in early 1942. *Below:* Early in the war, the shortage of weaponry was so acute that the United States armed its merchantmen with anything that would fire. Here, two members of the naval armed guard man an ancient, World War I–era Lewis machine gun.

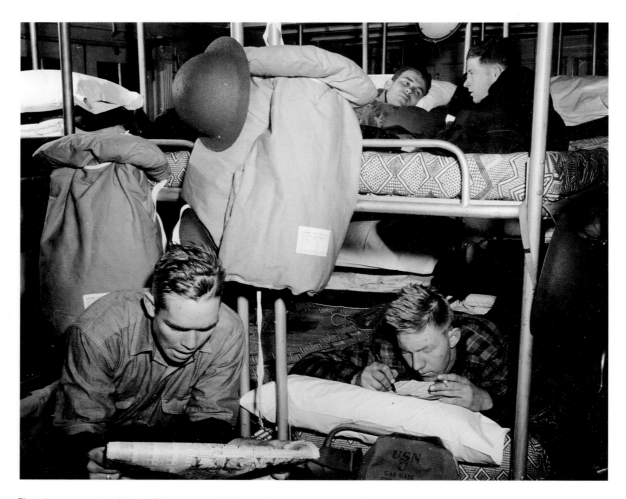

Above: Though not as cramped as the living spaces within the U-boats hunting them, life in the merchant marine was Spartan at best. Here, members of a cargo ship's crew relax in their very tight living quarters. *Below:* American shipyards were models of efficiency and good management. American yards had been laid out to take advantage of mass production techniques, which led to tremendous output during the war years.

Above: Some of the material of war that made it across the Atlantic. Trucks are unloaded at Liverpool Harbor. *Below:* Dozens of Jeeps await loading into cargo ships along New York's waterfront.

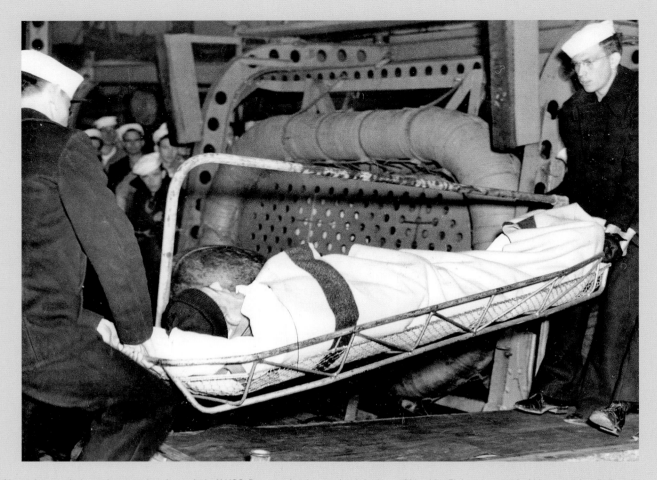

Above: A wounded merchant mariner is carried off USS *Broome* after he survived the loss of his ship. Eighty thousand of his comrades died at the hands of Germany's wolf packs. *Below:* An American blimp discovers the survivors of the Cuban freight SS *Libertad*, which was sunk by *U-123* off the North Carolina coast in 1943. Her crew survived on these rafts for thirty-six hours before being rescued by an American escort.

Above: Survivors of SS *Lancing*, a Norwegian whaler lost off Cape Hatteras on July 4, 1942, when she was torpedoed by Erich Topp's *U-552*. *Below:* Weary merchant mariners are bused to quarters ashore after being rescued by the U.S. Navy off the Virginia coast. On April 16, 1942, Reinhard Hardegen's *U-123* attacked their vessel, SS *Alcoa Guide*. Using their antiaircraft weapons, the crew of *U-123* killed or wounded most of the men on *Alcoa Guide*'s bridge. With her rudder jammed and her hull riddled, the American seamen abandoned ship. Hardegen ordered his men to cease fire as soon as the *Alcoa*'s crew hit their lifeboats. As a result, twenty-seven men survived the attack.

Above: While on route from Houston to New York, the tanker SS *Naeco* ran afoul of Johann Mohr's *U-124*. Filled with heating oil and kerosene, *Naeco* stood no chance against the Type IX boat. She was torpedoed with the loss of twenty-four of her thirty-eight crewmembers. *Right:* British merchant ship *Recorder* at sea in July 1942. She's carrying four LCMs (landing craft mechanized) strapped to her decks, plus a full cargo of supplies in her holds. No space was wasted on any merchant ship during those years, as every ton of material was needed on the far side of the Atlantic.

Above: Merchant sailors who survived the loss of their ship huddle in a lifeboat as they drift and pray for rescue. *Below:* A merchant mariner spotted from the air tries to climb into a raft dropped to him by a search-and-rescue aircraft.

Above: The Norwegian skipper of the SS *Lancing* describes the loss of his ship to Erich Topp's boat to a U.S. Navy intelligence officer following his rescue in July 1942. *Below:* A convoy seen from the gondola of an escorting U.S. Navy blimp. The Allies lost some thirty-six thousand sailors defending these convoys, while another thirty-six thousand merchant seamen went down with the nearly 3,500 vessels sunk by the Axis in the Atlantic.

CHAPTER ELEVEN

THE NIGHTMARE LOCUSTS

On June 22, 1941, the Germans invaded the Soviet Union, unleashing the bloodiest land war in history. Hundreds of thousands of soldiers and civilians died as the Wehrmacht battled its way east. Behind the lines came the execution groups, whose sole mission was to kill "undesirables." Mass killings wiped out most of the Jews in the Baltic states. The Waffen SS massacred entire towns in the Pripet Marshes.

The Red Army, caught by surprise, was chopped to ribbons during the first weeks of the war. Half-trained units fought and died in place; others were surrounded and forced to surrender. Those who survived faced life as slave laborers for the Nazi regime, then exile to the Siberian camps after the war.

The invasion destroyed tens of thousands of Russian aircraft and tanks, and it cost the Red Army more than a million casualties. Large swaths of the most industrialized sections of the Soviet Union fell into German hands. Production of weapons, aircraft, and tanks plunged. In desperation, the Russians disassembled threatened factories and sent them by rail to the safety of the Ural Mountains, where they were reassembled. The same workers who had manned those factories in the west were carted to the Urals as well, ensuring their special skills could continue to be used.

As the Red Army and Air Force fought and died in their motherland, Winston Chuchill and FDR extended support to their new, unlikely Allies. Churchill was the first to pledge support to the Soviet Union. As the Germans took Smolensk and began pushing toward Moscow, the British organized their first aid convoy, code-named Dervish. It set out in August 1941, six ships strong, to brave the harsh Arctic seas north of Norway.

At the time, this was the only route available to get war material to Russia. Starting from the convoy bases in Iceland, the Dervish ships traveled past Bear Island and steered east through the nightless Arctic skies to reach the Soviet port of Archangel. The six vessels offered token assistance at best—there were twelve Hawker Hurricanes crated aboard one cargo ship at a time when the Red Air Force had lost almost fourteen thousand aircraft—but the political message was clear: Britain would support Stalin.

The Soviets clamored for more. With their army on the ropes, the Germans less than three hundred miles from Moscow, and almost a million men in danger of being surrounded around Kiev, tokens of assistance meant little to them. They needed massive help, and they needed it quickly.

Opposite: The battleship USS *New York* escorting an Atlantic convoy. With the U.S. Navy committed to the Atlantic War by the fall of 1941, the British were able to free up surface assets to fulfill Churchill's promise of aid to Stalin.

The Luftwaffe all but crushed the Red Air Force in 1941. By December, the Germans had destroyed more than twenty-one thousand Russian planes. Aircraft from Britain and the United States became a crucial part of Allied Lend-Lease Agreement to the Soviet Union, making the Arctic convoys of supreme importance.

The British responded by organizing a regular convoy system from Iceland to Archangel and Murmansk. The first of these, PQ-1, sailed at the end of September with twenty-four heavily guarded merchant ships.

The convoy reached Russia without loss. Eight inbound and eight outbound convoys crossed the Arctic Ocean without any interception that year.

These early successes masked the potential for serious trouble. The Arctic run from Iceland required a four thousand–mile round trip through treacherous waters littered with ice flows. Much of the voyage took the convoys within shore-based aircraft range from Norway.

In February 1942, the Germans redeployed much of their remaining surface fleet from France to Norway in what became known as the Channel Dash. Right under the nose of the British, *Scharnhorst* and *Gneisenau*, escorted by the cruiser *Prinz Eugen* and six destroyers, reached Germany on February 13. *Gneisenau* was damaged and knocked out of the war by an air attack on Kiel a short time later. Meanwhile, *Scharnhorst* and *Prinz Eugen* headed to Norway. They were later joined by *Tirpitz* and other surface units, including *Admiral Scheer*, cruisers, and destroyers. Stationed within striking range of the Arctic convoy lanes, these ships represented a significant threat to the Allied effort to sustain Russia.

One of the first T-34 medium tanks to be encountered (and knocked out) by the Germans during the war in the east. During the first six months of fighting, the Nazi invasion cost the Red Army 20,500 tanks. In response, the Allies sent more than 12,000 tanks to the Soviets to help replace those losses.

By the spring of 1942, the Royal Navy was overwhelmed by its global commitments. In April, the same Japanese carrier force that set a torch to the Pacific swept into the Indian Ocean, sinking the Royal Navy carrier *Hermes*, two cruisers, and two destroyers. Almost as bad was the carrier *Ryujo*'s raid against merchant shipping in the Bay of Bengal, which destroyed twenty-three cargo vessels and wiped out much of the coastal traffic in the area.

Now, as the size of the Royal Navy was diminishing through such losses, it was expected to shoulder the burden in the Arctic as well. Given the level of the threat represented by the German capital ships and

Norway-based air power, each convoy to Russia required a Herculean commitment that tied up much of the Home Fleet.

As the German surface units gathered in Norwegian fjords, the Luftwaffe sent a combination of Stukas, Ju-88s, Heinkel He-111s, and Kondors to bases in the far north. Specializing in antishipping operations, these aircraft were crewed by experienced veterans who had taken a heavy toll on Allied shipping in the Atlantic and Mediterranean.

The days of the milk runs in the Arctic were over.

In early March, the Germans sent *Tirpitz*, sister ship of

(continued on page 215)

Above: General Lewis Brereton, then commander of the Ninth Air Force, laughs with a Soviet officer as they chat beside a Curtiss P-40 Warhawk destined for service in Russia. Thousands of P-40 Warhawks were sent to Russia during the war and were some of the earliest planes delivered by the Arctic convoys. *Opposite:* A Swordfish tail gunner snaps a photo of the escort carrier HMS *Chaser* shortly after takeoff during a run through the Arctic.

Above: The venerable Swordfish proved its versatility once again in the Arctic. Despite the terrible operating conditions, the old Stringbag gave the Royal Navy a sub-killing aircraft during each Arctic run. *Below:* The escort carriers HMS *Emperor* and *Striker* riding heavy Arctic swells. The Fleet Air Arm shined in such conditions and was able to launch aircraft in conditions no other navy could have operated in during the war.

As the Arctic convoys continued to strain the Royal Navy, losses in the Mediterranean piled up. In November 1941, *U-81* sank *Ark Royal* just thirty miles from Gibraltar. This left the British critically short of fleet carriers, forcing the Royal Navy rely on baby flat-tops for air support in the Arctic.

(continued from page 211)
the *Bismarck*, against convoy PQ-12. Escorted by three destroyers, the huge battleship hoped to intercept the convoy while evading the Royal Navy's two covering forces, which included three battlewagons and the fleet carrier *Illustrious*.

A British submarine screening PQ-12 detected the German force. Alerted to the *Tirpitz*'s sortie, the covering forces converged on her. In atrocious weather, the two sides had several near misses, and at one point were less than sixty miles from each other. But other than a straggler from PQ-12 that *Tirpitz*'s destroyers dispatched, they failed to locate each other. On March 9, 1942, the Germans turned for home, but were finally discovered by a search plane from *Victorious*. The carrier promptly launched a strike group of Fairey Albacore torpedo bombers (a biplane replacement for the venerable Swordfish). The attack failed to score a hit, and the German gunners downed two bombers.

This first indecisive encounter heightened the Admiralty's fear of *Tirpitz*. Had she been able to get into PQ-12, the close escort and the sixteen merchantmen would have stood no chance. A measure of paranoia developed around *Tirpitz* within the Royal Navy's leadership that would eventually contribute to the worst disaster of the campaign.

Meanwhile, PQ-12 made its way through the freezing waters, losing a whaler after so much ice built up on her decks that she capsized. The destroyer *Oribi* struck pack ice during the passage to Murmansk and was damaged as well.

Above: HMS *Penelope*, a light cruiser, seen at Malta. In 1942, the Royal Navy fought two campaigns of attrition outside the North Atlantic. The Arctic convoys and the effort to sustain Malta cost Great Britain much of her fighting navy. *Opposite above:* German aircraft savaged several Arctic convoys, prompting the British to include antiaircraft ships with the escort force in future runs. The best such platform available to the Royal Navy was *Dido*-class light cruisers like this one. Carrying ten 5-inch dual-purpose guns, plus a host of 20mm and 40mm auto cannons, they could throw walls of flak into incoming Luftwaffe dive and torpedo bomber formations. *Opposite below:* The Russians made good use of everything the Allies shipped to them. With the situation on the Eastern Front truly desperate from 1941 until late 1942, the Red Air Force in particular employed vast quantities of American and British aircraft. Here, a flight of P-40 Warhawks takes off for a winter mission.

Nearing the end of March, PQ-13 set out from Iceland in such arduous weather that the convoy had to be routed south of Bear Island to avoid ice flows. This put the Allied vessels even closer to the Luftwaffe's air bases in Norway.

On March 24, a massive storm struck the Arctic that scattered the convoy. The next day, the Luftwaffe detected and attacked the stragglers, sinking two ships.

On the twenty-sixth, a German destroyer force attempted to intercept the convoy. The conditions were so severe that spray sweeping over the British escorts' decks froze almost immediately. Gun wells filled with water as the warships pitched and rolled, and this soon froze. Ice coated everything—including the guns and torpedo tubes.

At 0900, the Germans made contact with the British escort force in fog and snow. In the chaotic encounter that followed, two Royal Navy destroyers engaged each other by accident and the cruiser HMS *Trinidad* was hit and damaged by one of her own errant torpedoes. Other attempts to launch torpedoes failed due to icing. By the end of the fight, German destroyer *Z-26* had been sunk, while the convoy proper had avoided harm. Over the ensuing days, the convoy lost three other ships before reaching Murmansk.

In early April, the next convoy, PQ-14, sortied in the midst of even worse weather and ice. Deep in the Arctic Ocean, the Allied sailors encountered thick fog and ice flows that damaged several of the escorts, forcing them to turn back. Soon, the convoy was scattered. Some of

Above: A Blohm & Voss Bv-142, one of four made for transatlantic mail service before the war. The Luftwaffe lacked suitable long-range patrol and attack aircraft during the war, a shortfall that cost the Germans dearly in both the Atlantic and in the Arctic. The Bv-142 was used briefly in France and Norway, but its operational record was poor and Bv-142s were withdrawn from service by 1942. *Below:* HMS *Victorious* played a major role in the convoy war in the Arctic. She is seen here at Hvalfjord, Iceland, prior to another escort mission to the far north in late 1941. By 1942, the defenses surrounding such convoys were multilayered and required complex planning to properly execute.

the cargo ships turned back. Others pressed on through the murk. In the midst of the weather, *U-403* attacked the convoy commodore's vessel, *Empire Howard* (6,985 tons). Laden with two thousand tons of war material plus a contingent of trucks for the Red Army, the *Empire Howard* sank in less than a minute. Miraculously, about half the crew survived, though the commodore was not among the rescued.

Every convoy inbound to Russia had to come out at some point. Those return voyages were no less hazardous in 1942. To maximize their protection, the Royal Navy synced each outbound convoy to the start of the inbound ones so that in the area of most danger—the waters near Bear Island—the two convoys would pass each other. This would allow the escorts and the covering forces to reinforce either convoy in case they were attacked. The outbound convoys from Murmansk and Archangel were designated QP.

At the end of April, PQ-15 and QP-11 entered the Arctic Ocean. The Germans tracked both and attacked with aircraft, U-boats, and marauding destroyers. The Royal Navy lost two destroyers and the cruiser *Edinburgh*, as well as four merchant ships from both convoys. The ferocity of the German attacks later caused the escort commander, Rear Adm. Stuart Bonham-Carter, to call for a suspension of the Arctic convoys: "The attacks will increase, not diminish."

He was right, but the political and military importance tied to the aid made it impossible to abandon. The Red Army had still not recovered from the losses of 1941.

It was short of everything from trucks and tanks to weapons and ammunition. Russia's factories needed raw materials to produce their own domestic designs, and the Red Air Force desperately needed Allied warplanes. Worse, the German summer offensive was set to begin in June. Churchill ordered the convoys be continued.

At the end of May, PQ-16 headed into the Arctic Ocean. In these northern latitudes, the sun shone twenty-four hours a day. Without darkness to conceal their movements, or keep them safe from the Luftwaffe, the convoy's ships came under constant air attack by swarms of Heinkels and Ju-88s.

Robert Carse, a merchant seamen on the Arctic run, wrote about such Luftwaffe attacks in his wartime memoir, *There Go the Ships*.

But here, all about, was destruction. Our column leader had just been struck by a bomb on the fore deck. It rent down through the port side and left a gaping hole twenty feet high. . . . There was a great, a horrible blast. She went in fifteen seconds, a blazing upward sheet of carmine, scarlet, and yellow that had the bite of acrid heat we could feel like a blow. The Nazis came back, low, right over the boats and rafts that somehow had lived to get away from what had been the ship.

They machine gunned those men . . . the men lay helpless and hunched. There was nothing they could do except keep still and die.

Based in Norway, the U-boats tasked with intercepting the Arctic convoys faced arduous operating conditions. Ice, freezing weather, and seas that drenched the surface watch with bone-chilling water made missions in the far north among the most difficult experienced by any of Doenitz's gray wolves.

Eight merchant ships went down: six to air attack, one to a U-boat, two more to mines. This represented about 20 percent of the convoy.

To get PQ-16 through, nearly fifty Allied warships took part in escorting it. Such strength required stripping other theaters, and after PQ-16 some of these ships had to be redeployed to the Mediterranean to help resupply Malta. Two of those ships, cruiser *Liverpool* and destroyer *Matchless*, were knocked out of action as a result of battle damage sustained on the Malta run. Additionally, another destroyer was sunk.

The run to Russia resumed on June 27, 1942, with the departure of PQ-17 from Iceland. Composed of thirty-six merchantmen, PQ-17 was protected by a combined Anglo-American group of escorts that included two U.S.

Navy cruisers and two destroyers. Distant support, to be called in if *Tirpitz* sortied, included the American battleship USS *Washington*, the British battlewagon *Duke of York*, carrier *Victorious*, two cruisers, and fourteen destroyers.

Closer to the convoy was the 1st Cruiser Squadron, composed of four cruisers and three destroyers. Their job was to fend off German destroyers attacks.

The antisubmarine warfare (ASW) and antiaircraft screen around the merchantmen included eight destroyers, four corvettes, and two antiaircraft ships. Given the losses being suffered by the Allies in the Atlantic and along American coastal waters, as well as in the Mediterranean and Pacific, PQ-17 represented a massive devotion of resources.

Above: The Dornier Do-18 was an older, less capable flying boat than the Do-24 that was used in Norway mainly as a search-and-rescue aircraft during the Arctic convoy battles. *Below:* A Dornier Do-24 flying boat. The Do-24 was used by the Luftwaffe units in Norway both as a reconnaissance aircraft and as a search-and-rescue platform. Only 279 were built during the war.

Above: The Heinkel He-111 medium bomber was adapted for the antishipping role by slinging aerial torpedoes beneath its fuselage. The crews were specially trained in a ship-killing torpedo tactic, known as the Golden Comb. Developed by KG-26 specifically for use against the Arctic convoys, the Golden Comb saw the geschwader form up in line abreast and attack a convoy from its front quarter. With each He-111 carrying two torpedoes, KG-26 could launch up to eighty weapons simultaneously. With so many torpedoes combing through a convoy, the Germans were almost certain to inflict damage. *Below:* A Heinkel He-111 crew inspects their survival gear prior to a mission. Getting shot down in the frigid Arctic Ocean was a virtual death sentence. In 1941 and 1942, the Luftwaffe and other German agencies conducted horrific experiments on concentration camp inmates at Dachau in hopes of understanding, preventing, and treating hypothermia. Cold-water immersion suits were developed as part of that effort. About a hundred inmates were killed during the course of the experimentation.

A Junkers Ju-88 mutlirole bomber going down in flames.

That summer, the code breakers at Bletchley Park were taking about twenty-four hours to decrypt the German navy's shark signals. As PQ-17 entered the most dangerous waters north of Norway, the Admiralty had no clear knowledge of where *Tirpitz* was. Had she sortied? First Sea Lord Adm. Dudley Pound fretted over what could happen to the convoy if the Germans successfully intercepted it with a battleship force.

On July 4 , Ultra decrypts revealed that the Luftwaffe was massing for an attack on PQ-17. The Admiralty signaled the convoy in the clear: "Most immediate, Blue Pendant. Blue Pendant." This was the code for incoming air attack. Sure enough, the sky filled with Ju-88s and Heinkel 111s, which sank an American freighter, damaged a Russian tanker, and forced two other ships to be scuttled.

That night, fearful that *Tirpitz* was at sea and about to reach PQ-17, the first sea lord intervened in the operation. At 2111 hours, he ordered the 1st Cruiser Squadron to withdraw. A few minutes later, a second signal reached PQ-17, ordering it to disperse. In an indication of clear panic emanating from the Admiralty, a third order arrived fast on the heels of the second one. This order, Pound's own decision, told PQ-17 to scatter.

At that point, it was every ship for herself.

The *Tirpitz* had, in fact, not yet sortied. Pound's decision, certainly an agonizing one to make, was the wrong call. And the merchant seamen in the Arctic paid the price for it.

The killing began the next morning. *Empire Byron*, which had been torpedoed by a KG-26 Heinkel 111 the previous day, was sunk by *U-703*. With her loss went

A Ju-88 crew during a bombing mission.

fifteen aircraft, thirty tanks, a half dozen other vehicles, and almost 2,500 tons of war material.

The American cargo ship *Honomu* went down that afternoon in the Barents Sea after running afoul of *U-456*. With 7,000 tons of tanks, steel, food, and ammunition in its holds and on deck, the *Honomu* sank stern first in less than ten minutes. Before *U-456* departed, her skipper gave the surviving Allied sailors food, an increasingly rare gesture of chivalry. Part of the crew who made it off *Honomu* drifted for almost two weeks before a British minesweeper picked them up. The others were not discovered until July 28, and then by a passing German U-boat. Eight of the original nineteen men in the boat were still alive. They'd been without food for almost a week. Eleven others had died of exposure, a grim and slow death to be sure.

One by one, the ships of PQ-17 were hunted down by aircraft and submarines. The convoy's rescue ship was blown out of the water during an air attack on the fifth.

Nine more merchantmen were sunk that day as well. By the time the bloodletting mercifully ended, only eleven vessels reached Russia. Twenty-three ships with more than a hundred thousand tons of vital war supplies had been destroyed. This included 210 aircraft, 430 tanks, and 3,350 trucks, jeeps, and other vehicles.

At first, the Soviets refused to believe so many ships could have been sunk. When it became clear what had happened, relations between the British and Russian deteriorated substantially, especially after an angry confrontation between Admiral Pound and the Soviet ambassador. The disaster also impacted relations with the United States. Admiral King, never fond of the British in the first place, was appalled at what had taken place. Soon after, he withdrew the U.S. Navy warships supporting the Arctic convoys and sent some of them to the Pacific.

After PQ-17, Churchill was forced to tell Stalin that there would be no further convoys to Murmansk or

Above: An Allied escort unleashes a depth-charge attack on a marauding German U-boat. The heavy seas, plus the presence of ice, made searching for submerged submarines very difficult, as such conditions diminished the effectiveness of ASDIC. *Below:* The Ju-88 was a fearsome opponent—fast, maneuverable, and capable of both level and dive bombing. Their crews destroyed vast amounts of Allied shipping in the Mediterranean and the Arctic.

Above: A U-boat crew in cold weather gear searches for targets on the far horizon. Operations in the harsh Arctic climate yielded only limited success for Doenitz's wolves. *Below:* Heading to sea at the start of another patrol.

The first Soviet military mission to reach Alaska poses beside its transport. They were the vanguard of a huge force of ferry pilots who flew American aircraft to Siberia, supplementing the aircraft sent via the Arctic convoys.

Archangel that summer. Nor would there be a second front opened to take the pressure off the Red Army. Stalin objected furiously. His nation's future hung in the balance, and with the German summer offensive driving on Russia's oilfields in the south, he needed the Allies' help more than ever before.

Reluctantly, Churchill agreed to send the next convoy in September. By then, though, the Royal Navy was in even more desperate shape. The Operation Pedestal convoys to Malta in August had cost the British an aircraft carrier, two cruisers, a destroyer, and nine merchant ships sunk, plus another carrier and two cruisers damaged. Resuming the Arctic convoys could only be done by stripping other commands. But it had to be done.

Convoy PQ-18 sailed for Russia from Loch Ewe, Scotland, on September 2, 1942. Its thirty-nine merchantmen, one rescue ship, three oilers, and three minesweepers were protected by layers of escort groups, each tasked with specific threats to counter. As part of ASW and antiaircraft defenses, three destroyers, four corvettes, two antiaircraft ships, and four ASW trawlers protected the convoy.

Another sixteen destroyers served as a screen against light German surface units. To fight Luftwaffe, the new escort carrier, HMS *Avenger* and its squadron of Hurricanes would stand guard. There was also a CAM ship in the convoy. *Avenger* also carried three ASW Swordfish.

Nine subs were assigned to watch the German fleet anchorages in Norway, and they could spot any sortie by the Kriegsmarine's heavy ships. In case they did sail, a distant cover force of two battleships with supporting cruisers and destroyers would be ready to intercept.

To furnish air cover for the convoy as it reached Russian waters, the Soviets allowed the British to base planes around Murmansk. Twenty-four bombers, a squadron of Catalina flying boats, and some photo recon Spitfires were now stationed there. Once again, the Arctic run required a massive outlay of planning, resources, and men.

(continued on page 232)

As part of Lend-Lease operations, the Royal Navy transferred a number of warships to the Soviet Union, including submarines HMS *Sunfish* and *Ursula* (tower visible in background).

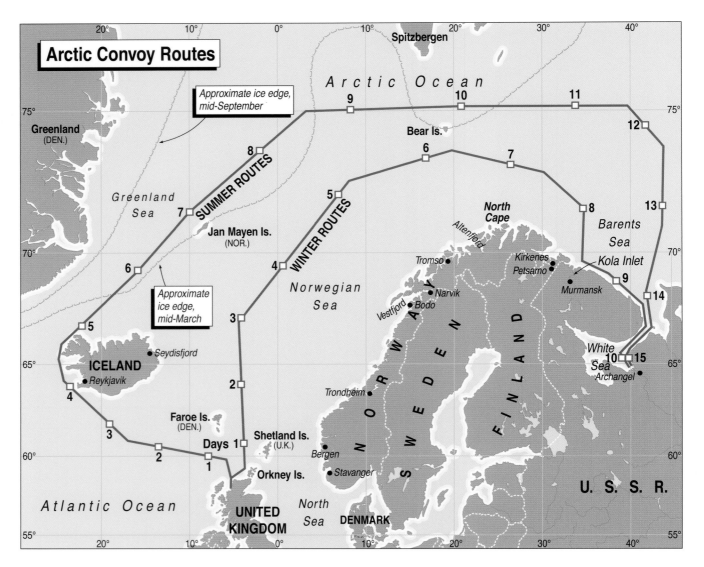

Arctic Convoy Routes

Approximate ice edge, mid-September

Approximate ice edge, mid-March

Arctic Ocean

Spitzbergen

Greenland (DEN.)

Greenland Sea

SUMMER ROUTES

Jan Mayen Is. (NOR.)

WINTER ROUTES

Bear Is.

North Cape

Altenfjord

Barents Sea

Kola Inlet

Norwegian Sea

Tromso

Kirkenes
Petsamo

Murmansk

Vestfjord
Bodo

Narvik

White Sea

Archangel

ICELAND

Seydisfjord

Reykjavik

Trondheim

N O R W A Y

S W E D E N

F I N L A N D

Faroe Is. (DEN.)

Days

Shetland Is. (U.K.)

Bergen

Stavanger

Atlantic Ocean

UNITED KINGDOM

North Sea

DENMARK

U. S. S. R.

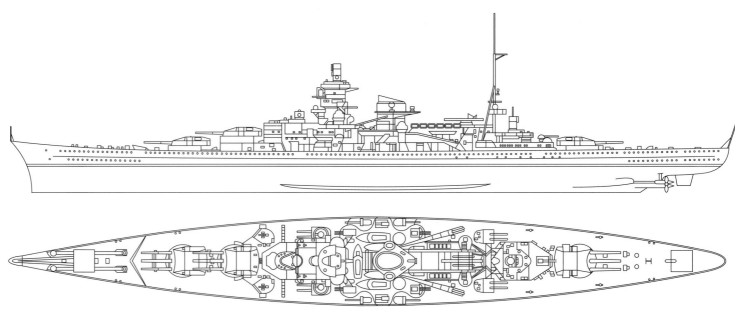

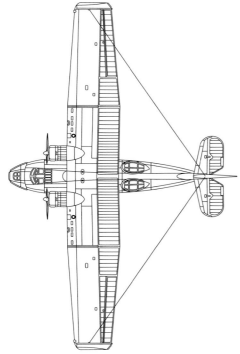

Opposite bottom: German battlecruiser *Scharnhorst* (pictured) with sister ship *Gneisenau* sank the aircraft carrier HMS *Glorious* and her two destroyer escorts on June 8, 1940. At the Battle of the North Cape, December 26, 1943, *Scharnhorst* was sunk by the *Duke of York* with support from destroyers *Scorpion* and *Stord* and cruisers *Belfast* and *Jamaica. The-Blueprints.com Above:* The Consolidated PBY-5A *Catalina* flying boat filled many roles in the war, including search and rescue, convoy escort, and anti-submarine warfare. *The-Blueprints.com Right:* The Focke-Wulf Fw 200 Condor also served multiple roles for the German Luftwaffe, including patrol bombing, reconnaissance, and troop transport. *The-Blueprints.com*

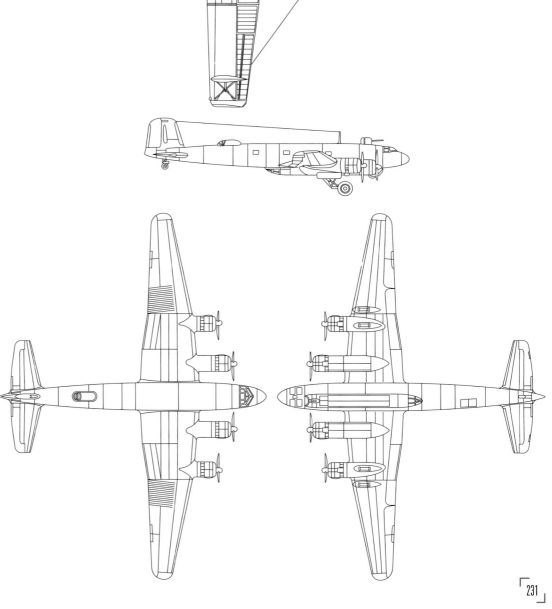

Scharnhorst, seen here with a U-boat, remained the principal surface raider threat to the Arctic convoys along with the battleship *Tirpitz*. Both warships tied down much of the Royal Navy's Home Fleet throughout 1942 and 1943 and forced the British to deploy capital ships in support of the Arctic convoys until both ships were finally sunk.

(continued from page 227)

On September 13, 1942, the attacks began. A wolf pack of nine boats had been stalking the convoy, though *U-88* had been sunk by escorts the day before. Now, *U-408* penetrated the ASW screen and sank the brand-new American cargo ship *Oliver Ellsworth* and the Russian freighter *Stalingrad*.

Later that day, forty Ju-88s and He-111s from KG-30 and KG-26—the Luftwaffe's premier antishipping units—bored in on the convoy. They hit PQ-18 with simultaneous dive-bombing and torpedo attacks. One British witness to the attack said they looked like "a huge flight of nightmare locusts."

In ten minutes, they sank eight ships.

At 0400 the next morning, *U-457* crippled *Atheltemplar*. Set afire by the torpedo hit, the 8,900-ton tanker drifted for hours after her crew abandoned her. Eventually she capsized, but her hull remained afloat until polished off by a few shots from *U-408*'s deck gun.

As the morning wore on, the Luftwaffe massed for the knockout blow. As the nightmare locusts returned, *Avenger*'s Hurricane squadron executed a perfect intercept. Without fighter escort, the German bombers were shot to pieces by the Hawkers.

Still, the Germans pressed their attack, only to find that the convoy escort had repositioned the antiaircraft ships to counter the threat. The AA cruiser *Ulster Queen* created a wall of flak, knocking down plane after plane.

The Germans refused to give up. They sent in two more attack waves. Each one suffered heavily and achieved little. By the end of the day, the two kampfgeschwaders had lost twenty-one aircraft. Even the CAM Hurricane got into the fight and scored a kill.

The running battle raged for four more days, but every German air and undersea attack was met with fierce resistance. By the time the convoy reached Murmansk,

During the Arctic runs, ice often formed on the Allied ships. In some cases, the additional weight of the ice proved so severe that it capsized vessels.

HMS *Nelson* under way in 1944. She was one of the few British modern battleships not to serve in the Arctic, having been committed to the Mediterranean theater. Her sister ship, the *Rodney*, joined the war in the Arctic in 1944.

thirteen merchants had been sunk. Twenty-eight had made it to Russia this time, and the German attacks had cost them three U-boats and forty-one bombers. The losses broke the back of the Luftwaffe's striking power in Norway. Air strikes against the Arctic convoys would never be as fierce or successful again.

The battle for PQ-18 was the turning point. Never again did the Germans threaten this vital sea lane to Russia, though in March 1943 the convoys were temporarily suspended so the escort force could join the fight in the North Atlantic. Prior to that, three more convoys had pushed through to Murmansk and Archangel.

By mid-1943, other routes to Russia had been opened. Material was flowing from Iran into southern Russia over a rail system built by the Western Allies. Massive aid was flowed in from the Pacific, where Japan's neutrality prevented the Imperial Navy from attacking the Russian convoys there. Aircraft also flew into Siberia in large numbers from bases in Alaska and the Aleutians. As a result, the Arctic route became less significant than during the crisis years of 1941 and 1942.

Nevertheless, in November 1943, the convoys resumed. The Germans, now on the defensive in Russia after having lost 650,000 men at Stalingrad, plus tens of thousands of more during the summer tank battles around Kursk, sought once again to stem the flow of aid to the Red Army. This time, instead of trying to choke off the supply route so the Wehrmacht could deliver the killing blow to Stalin's armies, destroying the Arctic convoys became a matter of survival for Germany. Every gun, tank, truck, and gallon of fuel delivered to Murmansk would help push the front lines closer to the Reich proper.

The surface threat from the Kriegsmarine had been substantially reduced by that fall, thanks to a British minisub attack on *Tirpitz* that knocked her out of the war until the spring of 1944. That left *Scharnhorst* as the primary threat.

THE COLD WAR
SELECTIVE MEMORY SYNDROME

The postwar tension between the United States and Soviet Union helped shape the historiography of World War II on both sides of the Iron Curtain. In the West, the victories in the Atlantic, North Africa, and Normandy were trumpeted as the war-winning campaigns that defeated the Nazi menace. In the Soviet Union, historians downplayed the Western Allies' involvement, focusing instead on the massive casualties suffered by the Russian people as they bled the German army to death on the Steppes.

After the fall of the Soviet Union, these one-sided views began to change, and the symbiotic nature of the alliance that won the war came into better focus. In Russia, researchers uncovered the extent and importance of Allied Lend-Lease aid. It was anything but the token support the Cold War politics and propaganda claimed. A closer look reveals how the Soviets were sustained by the aid so dearly delivered to Mother Russia:

- Aircraft: 20 percent of the Red Air Force's bomber units flew American or British planes. Sixteen percent of their front-line fighter units flew Allied aircraft, such as the Hurricane, the Thunderbolt, and the P-39 Airacobra. Soviet naval aviation was 29 percent Lend-Lease aircraft.

- Armor: In 1941 and 1942, after Russia lost 72 percent of their tanks during Operation Barbarossa, British and American armored fighting vehicles equipped 15 percent of Russia's vital tank forces.

- Trucks: The Russians received 351,000 trucks from U.S. and British factories. It is fair to say that the Red Army's incredible strategic mobility, which was put to such good use in the 1943 and 1944 campaigns, would not have been possible without these vehicles.

- Ammunition: Russia received 22 million artillery shells from American factories. That was equal to half domestic Soviet production.

- War Materiel: Chances were high that Red Army soldiers went into action wearing British- or American-made boots. Some fifteen million pairs were delivered to Russia during the war. More than 2.3 million tons of Lend-Lease steel reached Soviet factories, where it was forged into more tanks, weapons, and vehicles. Two hundred thirty thousand tons of aluminum kept the Soviet aviation industry in business, while almost four million tons of food helped feed the armies and the population. The Cold War skewed both sides' view of the victory in Europe. Perhaps in the years to come, a more holistic approach to the war will be possible.

The bottom line is, though, that without the Red Army, there never would have been a D-Day. Without Lend-Lease, there wouldn't have been a Red Army left capable of crushing the German Wehrmacht. The Allies needed each other, and it was Lend-Lease that bound them inexorably together.

Most Allied convoys making the run to Russia were supported by a screen of British submarines. They served as a scout line that could warn the convoy of any German raiders and also were the first line of defense against German destroyer sorties.

On December 20, 1943, convoy JW-55B sortied from Scotland, bound for Russia. After months of inaction and criticism from Hitler, the Kriegsmarine's surface force had an opportunity to score a significant victory if *Scharnhorst* intercepted the convoy. She sortied with a consort of destroyers on December 25, 1943.

Ultra decrypts revealed to the British that *Scharnhorst* had put to sea. The heavy cover force for the convoy, which included *Duke of York* and three cruisers, moved to protect the merchant ships. Bletchley Park's cryptographers were breaking Enigma signal traffic so quickly by this time that the heavy cover force commander was able to use the information they

provided to tactically position his warships to best counter *Scharnhorst*. It was an incredible advantage.

The weather deteriorated, forcing the German destroyers to return to base. *Scharnhorst* continued alone to make the attack on JW55B.

At 1615 hours on December 26, *Duke of York* and her heavy cruisers found the German battleship in abysmal weather. Despite the pitching seas, the Royal Navy's new radar-controlled fire direction system enabled *Duke* to score thirteen main gun hits on *Scharnhorst*. Heavy cruiser *Belfast*, plus several destroyers closed the range and pummeled her with shells and torpedoes.

The destroyer HMS *Sumarez* at sea. She led the attack on *Scharnhorst* in December 1943, scoring at least torpedo hits.

The German warship stood no chance. The British were at the top of their game after four years of continuous operations, while *Scharnhorst*'s crew, outnumbered and outgunned, had spent most of the war being part of the "fleet in being" but rarely setting out to sea.

The one-sided battle lasted for three hours until *Scharnhorst* finally capsized. Only thirty-six men out of her crew of almost two thousand survived to become prisoners of war.

After *Scharnhorst*'s loss, the remaining German surface warships became a nonfactor. Most were laid up or decommissioned or turned into floating batteries. *Tirpitz*, the last of the capital ships that had caused so much consternation for Churchill and the Royal Navy, was finally sunk by an RAF air attack in November 1944.

The Arctic convoys steamed to Russia for the rest of the war virtually unscathed. By May 1945, some 1,400 merchant ships had reached Murmansk and Archangel in a total of seventy-eight convoys. These brave merchant seamen delivered five thousand tanks, seven thousand aircraft, and almost four million tons of raw materials, trucks, tanks, ammunition, weapons, and fuel to the Soviet Union. This represented 23 percent of the total aid the Western Allies sent to Stalin during the war.

It came at a heavy price, especially in 1942. Total losses in the far north came to sixteen Royal Navy warships sunk (two cruisers, six destroyers, and eight escorts), plus eighty-five merchant ships. The Germans lost *Scharnhorst*, three destroyers, and thirty U-boats.

The mission was carried out. The Arctic sailors helped sustain the Soviet Union in its darkest hour. They paid with their blood for the message Churchill and Roosevelt conveyed to Stalin with every shipload

Left: British sailors work to clear expended shell casings away from their turret after a surface engagement. *Below:* Gunners from the *Duke of York*'s main battery pose aboard ship after sinking *Scharnhorst* in December 1943.

Above: A Russian merchant ship steams for Vladivostok after taking on a load of war material on the U.S. West Coast. As the war progressed, the Pacific run to Russia provided an increasing percentage of the Lend-Lease aid to the Soviet military machine, making the Arctic run less important than it had been in the dark hours of 1941 and 1942. *Opposite above:* Aerial reconnaissance photos show *Tirpitz* in a Norwegian fjord. The British attacked her repeatedly with air strikes and underwater demolition teams, finally sinking her in late 1944. *Opposite below: Prinz Eugen* seen in Trondheim Harbor after taking a torpedo hit from the Royal Navy submarine HMS *Trident* in 1942.

of supplies that reached Murmansk: Russia was not alone. For all their outlay of effort, lives, treasure, and assets, the Soviet Union did little to acknowledge the lengths to which the British and Americans went for it. At times derisive, always secretive and obstructionist, the Soviet regime made the sacrifice on behalf of the Russian people a bitter, but necessary pill to swallow.

And yet, the merchant crews continued to volunteer to go out time after time. There was no glory in what they did, nor was there fame. They died horrifically and anonymously in freezing weather thousands of miles from home, asking for little in return. In 1942, one of those veterans of the Arctic run wrote to a friend to explain why he had volunteered to crew another ship after his last one had been lost in the far north.

"Tonight makes two weeks since we came in, so it's about time for me to start looking for another ship. I wish that I could go out again with the blessed ignorance and expectation of high adventure that I did last time, but I'm afraid that's been knocked out of me. But I'll go back again, and again, to see swift death screaming down from the skies that I might one day come back to stay in peace in a land where men are free."

CHAPTER TWELVE

THE MEGA PACKS

By the fall of 1942, the Allies were fighting fires on every front. The defense of Stalingrad consumed the Russians in the east. In the Pacific, the Battle of Guadalcanal had turned into a pitched battle of attrition that had already cost the U.S. Navy and Australians dearly. In the Mediterranean, the Royal Navy had suffered brutal losses while trying to keep Malta from starving. In the Arctic, the convoys had just restarted after the PQ-17 nightmare. And in the main naval theater, the Atlantic, Adm. Karl Doenitz's U-boat strength climbed steadily. Production of new boats was running almost 20 a month in the second half of 1942. Doenitz possessed 121 operational boats in April, 285 total including the subs working up in the Baltic. By July, the number had grown to 140 operational, 331 total. Three months later, Doenitz fielded 196 with 365 in the fleet.

In August, as Operation Drumroll ended and the boats returned to the North Atlantic, the sub crews sank 131 ships in a bloodletting so fierce the number was only exceeded a handful of times during the war.

During September and October, the U-boat crews took out 236 vessels. Yet, with all this effort, the Germans were losing ground. They needed to be sinking at least 550,000 tons of shipping a month just to keep pace with new construction. Some months they achieved that, but most fell short.

To keep up the killing, Doenitz sent his boats farther and farther afield. In November, they sank 141 ships, many of which were independents sailing alone off South Africa. While such losses were cumulative and served to wear the Allies down, they did not produce decisive results.

The convoys would be the deciding factor. If the Germans could find a way to negate the defensive power of the convoy and undermine the entire value of the system itself, a decisive victory might have resulted.

In early November, the type of massed attack unleashed on convoy SC-107 looked to be the key to that German victory. The convoy had sailed from New York on October 24, 1942, initially protected by the Western Local Escort Force. On October 30, the convoy rendezvoused with Canadian group C-4, which was part of the Mid-Ocean Escort Force. That same day, *U-522* detected it and radioed its position to a pack of thirteen boats. As SC-107 steamed deeper and deeper into the North Atlantic, the escort group sparred with the first boats to make contact. Patrol planes sank two of the boats as they converged on the convoy.

Opposite: By 1943, there was no stopping the United States' ship-building industry. New cargo ships joined the fight almost hourly as production was ramped to a fever pitch. Even with his three hundred U-boats, Doenitz stood no chance of winning the tonnage war once America's industrial might was fully harnessed.

Even as Doenitz's Operation Drumroll ravaged American coastal traffic, the United States still managed to execute its first offensive of the war. The invasion of Guadalcanal in August 1942 triggered a campaign that would ultimately claim dozens of warships and tens of thousands of sailors, soldiers, and marines from both sides.

On November 1, 1942, part of the convoy's escort force turned for home to refuel. That left C-4 with five escorts to face eleven, later reinforced to thirteen, U-boats. The Canadians brilliantly drove off several attacks that day, but after midnight, the pack bored in and overwhelmed SC-107's defenders. They torpedoed twelve ships before dawn and then stalked the convoy as it limped through the black pit of the mid-ocean air gap. Over the next two days, seven more ships were sunk or damaged out of a convoy totaling forty-two vessels. On November 5, SC-107 reached the operational radius of aircraft from Iceland, and the first Liberators arrived to drive off the remaining U-boats pursuing the convoy.

Altogether, SC-107 lost fifteen ships sunk, four damaged. This represented more than a hundred thousand tons sunk or knocked out of action for the Allies in one two-day period. If the Germans could continue to effect such interceptions, the tide could be turned in their favor.

Despite the staggering losses—the Axis sank more than seven hundred thousand tons of shipping that month—there were encouraging signs for the Allies. Most important, on November 7, 1942, the U.S. and British launched their first joint offensive of World War II, dubbed Operation Torch. Designed to clear the Germans, Vichy French, and Italians out of Northwest Africa with

A British minelayer burns in Malta's Valletta Harbor. While the Allies fought fiercely in the Atlantic, Arctic, and Guadalcanal, the pivotal convoy battles to Malta raged on through August 1942.

a series of amphibious landings in Morocco and Algeria, Torch became the first and only transcontinental invasion launched during the war when most of the units involved sailed from American ports. Hundreds of ships, bulging with troops and supplies, steamed across the mid-Atlantic and encountered no significant opposition from Doenitz's men. As brutal as the convoy battles were in the Atlantic that November, the U-boats could not deny the Allies the strategic flexibility needed to pull off the first Anglo-American offensive of the war.

The Christmas season brought little joy to the men plying the North Atlantic. With B-Dienst decrypting Royal Navy Cipher No. 3, the Germans not only possessed

an accurate picture of the convoy situation in the North Atlantic, but they were also able to read the British situation reports on known U-boat concentrations. From those, Doenitz could anticipate where the Allied convoys would be routed and redeploy his packs to patrol those areas.

Just after the holiday, the Germans gave the Canadians and British another taste of what could happen in 1943 when the winter weather relented. Convoy ONS-154 was set upon by no fewer than nineteen U-boats. Its Canadian escort group, C-1, included only one destroyer and five corvettes. The Canadian vessels were universally outdated, lacking radar and crewed by men hastily

Top: After dropping depth charges, a Catalina of 333 Squadron, a Norwegian-crewed RAF squadron, exchanges fire with a U-boat while on patrol. The badly damaged aircraft made it back to its base in Scotland but sank after landing. *Chris Sheppard Above:* U.S. Army Rangers during Operation Torch, the first Anglo-American offensive against the Axis powers. Torch was the only transcontinental amphibious assault of the war. Despite the Rangers having to cross the Atlantic from the United States, Doenitz's U-boats failed to intercept and stop the invasion forces.

British freighters taking on a load of crated aircraft at an East Coast port in late 1942. The Battle of the Atlantic would reach a climax early in 1943.

trained for the most technically demanding work at sea. Despite these handicaps and being outnumbered four-to-one by Doenitz boats, the Canadian ships put up a valiant fight, sinking *U-356* with depth charges in a well-coordinated attack.

One down, only eighteen to go. The task was too large for the forces at hand. The Canadians were swamped, and from December 26 to 30, ONS154 came under constant attack. The U-boats destroyed or damaged twenty-six of ONS154's forty-five ships—over half the convoy.

The attack reinforced Allied fears that brute force could overwhelm the convoy system. If that happened, there weren't any options to replace it that could keep losses down. The entire future of the Allied cause lay in the convoy system.

But what were the Allies to do? In January 1943, they had less than half of the escorts needed to give every convoy solid protection. With the available ones so stretched, the Allies had no hope of achieving equality of numbers after a pack homed in on a convoy. Only

Above: A Douglas SBD Dauntless dive bomber is readied aboard the *Ranger* for a mission off the North African coast during Operation Torch.
Opposite: The SBD Dauntless served as an excellent carrier-based ASW aircraft during operations in the Atlantic and off the North African coast. They were later replaced by the even more capable TBM Avenger, which became the Navy's primary ship-based sub killer from 1943 until the end of the war.

by sending reinforcements to U-boat-plagued convoys could the weight of numbers be countered, but that was hit or miss. The reinforcements were generally dispatched after a convoy was hit, which gave the U-boats at least a night to wreak their havoc. In this equation, as long as U-boat production increased, Doenitz had the upper hand. The coming spring would determine the outcome of the war.

Doenitz started the New Year with three hundred operational boats and a promotion. After the surface fleet failed to press an attack on a convoy in the Arctic Ocean, Hitler called Admiral Raeder to his headquarters and harangued him on the uselessness of his capital ships. He told Raeder he intended to decommission

the remaining ships and use their guns as coastal defense batteries. This was too much for the old admiral, who resigned.

Hitler gave Doenitz command of the Kriegsmarine. In a series of conferences with Hitler, he convinced his master to hold off on dismantling the surface warships, since they were still capable of tying up much of the Royal Navy as a "fleet in being." At the same time, all the pieces had finally fallen into place. He had the three hundred boats he had wanted prior to the war's onset. From late January on, B-Dienst was supplying him with excellent intelligence, and his boats were crewed by capable men. They were poised to turn the tide.

(continued on page 252)

Above: The escort carrier USS *Chenango* was loaded with a full group of U.S. Army Air Force P-40 Warhawks, which the baby flat-top launched off the North African coast during Operation Torch. The army pilots then flew to bases ashore. Such strategic flexibility would not have been possible had the U-boat menace not been kept at bay during the invasion. *Opposite:* A series of photos showing U-boats under construction in Germany. By early 1943, the Germans had mastered the art of mass-producing U-boats using prefabricated sections constructed in different locations and then sent to assembly plants by rail. Such techniques allowed the production rate to skyrocket, giving Doenitz the three hundred boats he'd wanted for so long.

Above and opposite: One of the more unusual patrol and ASW aircraft to see service during the Atlantic campaign was the Consolidated PB2Y Coronado. Conceived as a long-range patrol aircraft, the production model lacked the operational radius of the PBY and was not widely employed as a result. It was used briefly in the Atlantic until leaking fuel tanks and other issues caused it to be withdrawn from combat units.

(continued from page 248)

First, the weather had to cooperate. January 1943 saw the Atlantic's worst weather of the war. Finding the convoys in the churning ocean, through storms and snow flurries, became an almost impossible task. At the same time, after months of blackout following the Kriegsmarne's adoption of the Shark code and the four-rotor Enigma, Bletchley Park's mad geniuses finally started cracking Doenitz's signals again. This gave the Allies enough insight to U-boat locations that many of the convoys were successfully routed away from the packs. During the entire month, the one hundred boats on patrol in the Atlantic managed to sink forty-four ships, almost all of which were stragglers or independents.

There was one exception. On January 3, 1943, convoy TM-1 from Trinidad bound for Gibraltar encountered *U-514* west of the Azores. The escort commander was ordered by the Admiralty to change course and route around a known patrol line of U-boats. This was Doenitz's Group Dolphin, composed of eight boats. The escort commander refused, as it would have denied him the ability to refuel his warships in less harsh seas. It was a dreadful tactical error.

On January 7, 1943, TM-1's nine tankers were set upon by Group Dolphin. The single destroyer and three corvettes in the escort force were overwhelmed, just like what happened with ONS154.

Seven of the nine tankers went down, taking more than one hundred thousand tons of fuel, a loss so severe

that the British had ration gas by another 10 percent.

The climactic battles of the Atlantic War began at the end of January when Doenitz's men intercepted convoy HX-224, touching off a series of pitched engagements that lasted through the next three months.

On January 29, 1943, HX-224 was detected and attacked by five U-boats in terrible weather. Defended by Canadian escort group C-4, HX-224 lost three ships to sub attacks. The crew of *U-632* rescued one of the Allied sailors whose vessel had been shot out from under him, and during his interrogation he revealed there was another convoy right behind HX-224.

This was slow convoy SC-118. Composed of sixty-one ships, her departure from port was detected by B-Dienst. Combined with the information revealed by the captured

sailor, the Germans had a pretty good idea where SC-118 was. U-boat Group Pfeil, composed of thirteen subs, was ordered to intercept, along with five more from Group Haudegen. Two other boats that had attacked HX-224 also set off in pursuit.

Facing these twenty submarines was British escort group B-2, composed of three destroyers, four corvettes, and a U.S. Coast Guard cutter. Once again, the Allied warships protecting their charges would be seriously outnumbered.

In the early morning of February 4, 1943, *U-187* was patrolling on the surface when a star shell exploded in the distance and revealed SC-118 to the sub's watch. It was a tragic error—an exhausted merchant seamen had accidentally fired the projectile, and it triggered one of the

Above *left:* Reinhard Hardegen, skipper of first *U-147* then later *U-123*, sank twenty-two vessels during his career. He took part in two Operation Drumroll patrols during 1942, where he and his crew destroyed more than a hundred thousand tons of Allied shipping. As of 2012, he is one of the last U-boat aces still living. *Above Right:* Erich Topp, Germany's third-ranking U-boat ace, survived the war to write his memoirs and serve in the postwar navy. He retired as a two-star admiral and died in 2005. *Below left:* Topp earned the Knight's Cross with Oak Leaves and Swords on August 17, 1942, for his depredations in the New World during Operation Drumroll. He completed twelve war patrols during the course of his career. *Below right:* By spring of 1943, U-boat crews knew the odds were stacked against them. Their morale dropped. British intelligence detected it, and the Allies exploited it by launching a devastating counter-offensive against Doenitz's men.

USS *George W. Ingram* slides down the way at the Bethlehem yard in Hingham, Massachusetts. Built and commissioned in seven months, the destroyer escort went into action in October 1943.

most hard-fought naval battles of the Atlantic campaign.

Commanded by Kapitänleutnant Ralph Muennich, *U-187* was a new Type IXC boat on its first patrol. Muennich quickly radioed a contact report to Doenitz's headquarters, which sent the rest of Group Pfeil scrambling to reach the convoy. At the same time, the escort around SC-118 detected the radio transmission and pinpointed it with their HF/DF (HuffDuff) radio direction finding gear. Two escorts broke formation and raced for the contact location. They located the German sub and sank her with the loss of nine men killed, forty-five captured.

Throughout the night and morning, four U-boats

made attempts to penetrate the screen and get to the convoy. But escort group B-2 was an experienced unit, though several new warships had recently joined the veterans. Normally under the command of Cmdr. Donald Macintyre, B-2 had a sterling reputation as one of the best sub hunters in the Royal Navy. During this engagement, however, Macintyre was in England and his executive officer, Lt. Cmdr. Francis Proudfoot, directed B-2 during this fight.

He and his men did an admirable job, blocking every German move to penetrate the screen. During the fighting, the convoy made a course change, but part of it failed to execute the maneuver. For several tense

A U-boat under air attack somewhere in the Atlantic. As the mid-ocean air gap was closed with the arrival of large numbers of escort carriers, the U-boats found few remaining safe havens when operating on the surface.

hours on the morning of February 5, 1943, B-2 had to try to protect a divided force. Not only did they succeed, but they damaged *U-609* in the process.

Later that day, the two parts of the convoy reunited, though a U-boat picked off a straggler as the weather deteriorated. Given the amount of radio traffic emanating from around SC-118, the Allied high command knew the convoy was in serious trouble. They began to send reinforcements, and three American escorts, based out of Iceland, raced south to link up with the B-2.

For a short time, the weather threw off the pursuit. In the wild waves and sheets of rain, Doenitz's gray wolves sought to regain contact with this plum target, but it was not until February 6 when *U-465* sighted SC-118 that the Germans were able to home in on their prey again. *U-465* paid the price for broadcasting

a contact report. HuffDuff picked up the transmission, and a Liberator hunted *U-465* down and severely damaged her.

The boats sank another straggler trailing behind SC-118 before launching a six-boat attack on the night of February 6. Proudfoot's able sub hunters parried every attack and managed to inflict serious damage on *U-267*, which broke contact and limped eastward, reaching St. Nazaire on February 18, 1943.

As the fighting raged, the escorts left one side of the convoy exposed while they dealt with multiple contacts on the other side. This allowed *U-262* to make an attack that sank one small cargo ship, which went down with all hands. In the predawn darkness, *U-402*—commanded by Kapitänleutnant Siegfried von Forstner, one of the best and most aggressive U-boat skippers still alive by 1943—*U-402* sank two more ships out of the convoy, causing so much confusion that B-2 lost control of the situation. One of Forstner's victims was SC-118's rescue ship, the loss of which meant that Proudfoot's escorts now had to pull survivors out of the water while simultaneously chasing down contacts.

Forstner, who had served aboard *U-99* under Silent Otto Kretschmer, ran riot in the chaos. Altogether, he and his crew torpedoed seven ships, while *U-608* destroyed two more. In return, the Free French corvette, her skipper, and crew displaying considerable elan, chased down *U-609* and rammed her. As the sub dived, the plucky corvette finished her off with depth charges. None of *U-609*'s crew survived.

An RAF Flying Fortress patrolling over the convoy on February 7 spotted and destroyed *U-624*, bringing Doenitz's losses to three U-boats sunk, four damaged.

Seven of the twenty engaged became casualties, while twelve Allied ships had gone down, plus one more damaged. Doenitz later wrote that he considered this one engagement the hardest-fought of the Atlantic war.

Doenitz wanted tonnage, and he didn't care where it came from. As far as he was concerned, an empty ship heading to America was just as good a target as one laden with tanks for Russia. This is why in mid-February, he ordered eighteen of his boats to converge on the forty-nine ships of ONS-166. Protected by escort group A-3, which was led by a U.S. Coast Guard officer named Cmdr. Paul Heineman, ONS-166 was an outbound convoy running between England and the United States.

Ultra picked up the concentration and the convoy was rerouted to try and avoid it. Not long after that order was sent to ONS-166, B-Dienst decrypted it and passed the course changes to Doenitz. He rerouted his boats,

A Royal Navy *Black Swan*–class sloop of war, one of the most successful ASW vessels designed and built by the British during World War II. Thirty-seven of these vessels were built between 1939 and 1945, and they were credited with sinking twenty-nine U-boats. Commander Frederic John "Johnnie" Walker, the Royal Navy's best sub-killing skipper, used his *Black Swan*–class sloop (the *Starling*) to help sink eleven U-boats. Armed with six 4-inch guns, plus depth charges and later Hedgehogs, they could make twenty knots, fast enough to overtake a surfaced Type VIIC U-boat.

The 2nd Escort Group, commanded by "Johnnie" Walker, became the highest-scoring ASW team of the war. Credited with destroying twenty-three boats in two years, the 2nd included the ships pictured here: HMS *Loch Fada*, *Wren*, *Domimica*, and *Loch Killin*.

and on February 20, 1943, *U-604* made first contact that afternoon. The sub radioed the convoy's location and then was driven down by one of Heineman's escorts.

But the contact report set the gray wolves on the convoy's trail. The eighteen U-boats sent against the convoy gradually burned through Heineman's escort force, which included two Coast Guard cutters and five *Flower*-class corvettes.

From February 21 through February 24, the onslaught claimed ship after ship. The escorts raced back and forth, furiously prosecuting the boats they detected, but at times so many came after the convoy simultaneously, that they just could not stop every attack run. Two subs

were destroyed by patrolling aircraft, and the cutter Campbell rammed and sank *U-606*. But the battle whittled down the number of escorts, as several had to break contact to refuel in Iceland. Plus, the Campbell was damaged so severely by the ramming that she had to leave as well. A Polish destroyer arrived to add her guns to the fight, but the slaughter continued. When the battle mercifully ended, fourteen merchant ships totaling 88,100 tons had been sunk. Seven more ships were damaged—almost 50,000 tons worth.

As these pivotal battles brought the war in the Atlantic to its climax, the senior naval leaders from the United States, Canada, and Great Britain gathered

Top-scoring U-boat Commanders of World War II

#	Commander	Patrols	Ships Sunk	Tonnage
1	Otto Kretschmer	16	47	273,043 tons
2	Wolfgang Lueth	15	46	225,204 tons
3	Erich Topp	12	35	197,460 tons
4	Heinrich Liebe	9	34	187,267 tons
5	Viktor Schütze	7	35	180,073 tons
6	Heinrich Lehmann-Willenbrock	10	25	179,125 tons
7	Karl Friedrich Merten	5	27	170,151 tons
8	Herbert Schultze	8	26	169,709 tons
9	Günther Prien	10	30	162,769 tons
10	Georg Lassen	4	26	156,082 tons

Left: A U-boat crew eating chow in their dismal, cramped quarters.

Below: To further bolster the ASW defenses in the South Atlantic, the United States provided the Brazilian armed forces with Consolidated PBY Catalina patrol bombers. The Brazilians put them to good use, sinking *U-199* in July 1943.

Opposite: The PB4Y-1 Liberator was a pivotal addition to the Atlantic campaign. With its incredible radius of action, heavy armament, and bomb load, these aircraft became the backbone of the very long-range patrol bomber force. Liberators were credited with seventy-two U-boat kills during the war. *Above:* A U-boat crew practicing with its antiaircraft armament. Doenitz originally believed he could deal with the increased air threat to his boats by arming them with quadruple AA guns. These were fitted later in 1943, replacing the single-barreled 20mm or 37mm guns typically mounted on Type VIIC and Type IX boats.

for what became known as the Washington Convoy Conference. It ran during the first two weeks in March, and while no overall command was established to run the antisubmarine effort, there were some important decisions made that restructured how the Allies would prosecute the campaign for the rest of the war. First, the Canadians were given their one and only command of World War II. This was the Canadian Northwest Atlantic Zone, headed by Rear Adm. Leonard Murphy, and it made Canada an equal partner in the war against the U-boats. The Canadians were supposed to focus on this area, which ran from just north of New York out to forty-seven degrees west. This meant pulling the Canadian

escort groups from the Mid-Ocean Escort Force (MOEF) and turning over that responsibility to the Royal Navy. Part of this was vindictiveness on the part of the British, who blamed the Canadian MOEF groups for many of the losses suffered over the past several months. In fact, 80 percent of the recent shipping losses in the North Atlantic had been incurred on convoys escorted by the Canadian groups. But the reasons for this were not Canadian ineptitude, as the British intimated on more than one occasion. The quality of the Canadian escorts simply did not pass muster by 1943. Using outdated weapons and sailing into action with obsolete technology—lacking even basic radar systems—was not a recipe for success.

THE DENIZENS OF BLETCHLEY PARK

I shivered at seeing the actual words of the signals passing between Admiral Doenitz and the boats under his command whose terrible work I had seen at first hand.
—Edward Thomas, boarding party for the captured *U-570*

Edward Thomas's reaction as he eavesdropped on his enemy preparing to kill as many of his family, friends, and countrymen as possible was visceral. Thomas was a British naval officer and intelligence analyst at Bletchley Park, source of the Ultra intelligence. On the U-boat war, he described, he added, "No less shocking was the revelation of the bestiality that underlay this sophisticated form of warfare. This emerged vividly from Doenitz's exhortations to his captains—'Kill, kill, kill'—and the names given to the wolf packs, such as Gruppe Blutrausch (Blood Frenzy)." Knowledge of the enemy's violent intentions and Britain's very survival at stake galvanized Bletchley Park's diverse contingent of officers, civilians, professors, secretaries, academics, and entrepreneurs. Knowing that countless lives depended on their work created a pressure cooker atmosphere, yet at the same time forged a unique culture that the veterans of Bletchley would never forget.

On arriving for his first day as an intelligence analyst, Telford Taylor remembered, "I cannot adequately portray the warmth and patience of the HUT 3 denizens." Many of the Bletchley Park civilians felt the need to defend their contribution to the war effort to outside friends and acquaintances who questioned why they were not in uniform. Their work so vital and yet their secret so dark, they could say nothing that even hinted at their purpose. On a site visit to Bletchley Park in September 1941, Winston Churchill referred to them as "the geese that lay the golden eggs and never cackle."

Secrecy was so high that in one case a husband and wife both worked at Bletchley Park and didn't know it.

They only discovered their secret after the war when they received separate invitations to a Bletchley reunion.

Every employee was told that from the first moment until their dying day they were not to even hint at their work. They were all required to sign the Official Secrets Act. The secret lasted until 1974 when F. W. Winterbotham published *The Ultra Secret*, which many Bletchley Park veterans considered a betrayal of their oath of silence.

Bletchley Park included fifty-five acres of offices, work spaces, and huts. A hut was a group of small, wooden buildings assigned to a functional task. Each hut was given a number. They were dilapidated-looking structures surrounded by blast walls, but inside some of the West's most creative geniuses performed miracles of mathematics, science, and computing.

Alan Turing, the father of computer science, was the head of Hut 8. Hut 8 received the German navy transmissions and performed the initial decryptions. Hut 8 paired with Hut 4, which turned the raw decryptions into usable intelligence, prioritized the information, and then forwarded it to the Admiralty. Working from a device that the Polish delivered to Bletchley, Turing developed the electromechanical "bombe" machine to iteratively solve for the set of rotors used, their order, and the keys each day. Breaking the codes once was not enough. They had to be broken each day as the Germans changed them, an exceptional task at times when there were no captured codebooks available.

Hut 6, headed by famed cryptanalyst Gordon Welchman, received German army and air force transmissions. These raw decryptions were forwarded to Hut 3 for translation into valuable intelligence. Welchman, who would later teach the first computing course at the Massachusetts Institute of Technology, made a significant improvement to Turing's "bombe" in

1940. His enhancement, known as the diagonal board, increased the speed at which enigma settings could be tested and codes cracked. Turing and Welchman were among the first four recruits, along with Stuart Milner-Barry and Hugh Alexander, and came to be known as the "Wicked Uncles of Bletchley Park."

The huts carried out their individual charters but worked together for deadly effectiveness. Hut 8 and Hut 6 were both using the same bombes in Hut 11, of which there were eighty by the end of the war, which meant that they had to prioritize which messages were decrypted first in near real time. The U-boat messages often got priority since so many lives and Britain's ability to fight the war were at stake.

In their efforts to accomplish their goal by whatever means necessary, they were sometimes a picture of contradiction. In cracking codes, they used some of the most advanced mathematics, computing algorithms, and electromechanical machinery known. But to send messages between Hut 6 and Hut 3 without getting wet in the rain, they used a primitive tray with a string that traveled in a tunnel between the two buildings. The sender would rattle a broom handle to alert the other side to pull the string and retrieve the message.

Every member of the diverse team at Bletchley Park was singularly focused on fighting the intelligence war. Without the close cooperation and constant teamwork across specialized functions both within Bletchley Park and with the military, the code-breaking efforts would have been fruitless. Messages had to be decrypted, translated, placed into military context, and forwarded to the people who could use the information to strategic and tactical advantage before it was too late. By the end of the war, there were thousands of people coordinated in this process and sworn to the deepest secrecy to keep Britain alive.

—*Allison Serventi Morgan*

In 1943, the Royal Navy started sending surface task forces into the Bay of Biscay to further disrupt Kriegsmarine operations from French ports. At the end of December, a pair of British cruisers, *Glasgow* and *Enterprise*, intercepted a force of German destroyers, sinking three and damaging four others without loss. This photo was taken aboard the *Glasgow* during that engagement, which was the last major surface engagement of the European war.

The Canadians had been given second-rate equipment as a stop gap during the desperate days of 1941 and 1942, but starting in the spring of 1943 they began to receive the latest technology. And as Doenitz would soon find out, that technology made all the difference in the war against his gray wolves.

The U.S. Navy was assigned the Central and South Atlantic, and the Tenth Fleet would be responsible for providing the escorts for the Eastern Sea Frontier and all the transcontinental convoys running between the United States and North Africa. This meant the United States would withdraw from the North Atlantic, leaving the nautical pipeline to England entirely to the Royal Navy.

While the admirals debated the restructuring from the comfort of D.C. conference rooms, the situation in the Atlantic became critical. At the start of March, Doenitz had pushed seventy boats into the North Atlantic. Never had the Allies faced this level of power before, and it came just as the Germans changed their U-boat weather code. The change blinded Bletchley Park, whose code

The U.S. Coast Guard cutter *Spencer* saw extensive combat during the climactic convoy battles in the first quarter of 1943. Here, she depth charges *U-175* after the Type VIIC sub attacked convoy HX-233 on April 17, 1943. The depth-charge attack crippled the sub, wrecking some of its batteries, which released deadly chlorine gas into the compartment. A second salvo of depth charges cracked the boat's pressure hull and forced her to the surface.

breakers couldn't read the key to the operational signal traffic as a result. The code names on the U-boat grid maps also changed constantly, making it even hard to figure out where Doenitz had deployed his boats. In February, the Bletchley Park folks could break key signals within twenty-four hours. Now, in March, it was taking days, sometimes weeks. In the middle of the month, there was a period of complete blackout at a crucial juncture in the fighting.

Conversely, B-Dienst was reading so many signals from the Royal Navy traffic that they were pinpointing convoys for Doenitz at an unprecedented rate. As a result, the U-boats intercepted every single North Atlantic convoy for two weeks, half of which were attacked. In the ensuing carnage, 22 percent of the ships sailing never reached their destinations. If these losses continued, the Germans would surely severe the logistical pipeline between the New World and Europe.

The worst moments for the Allies began when Doenitz sent twenty-seven boats against the fifty-nine ships in convoy SC-121. The convoy was protected by "Heineman's Harriers—escort group A-3, which by then consisted of the U.S. Coast Guard cutter *Spencer*, destroyer USS *Greer*, and two Royal Navy and two Canadian corvettes. The USS *Campbell* was still out of action after her ramming incident the previous month, which left A-3 not only short-handed, but working with new ships whose crews had not trained together. Worse, the escorts that had been with Heineman during the ONS-166 fight in February had not received any refit, crew rest, or repairs. Their sensors, weapons, and ships were far from peak shape as a result. Such was the desperate shortage of escorts that March that the Allies were forced to overwork the men and ships they did have. The cost for such extreme measures was paid in blood and treasure.

Two remarkable shots of *U-175* showing the damage inflicted by the depth-charge attack.

After *U-175* broke the surface, the USS *Spencer* sent a boarding party across to her in hopes of securing valuable codebooks or other intelligence. As the surviving crew abandoned ship, the boarding party reached the conning tower (pictured here), but it could not get inside the sub as it was sinking too quickly.

On March 6, 1943, *U-405* detected the convoy. For the next five days, the twenty-seven boats laid waste to the SC-121. Heineman's ships had no chance to protect their charges, and by March 10, fourteen ships had gone down and another one was damaged. The onslaught cost the Allies well more than sixty thousand tons of shipping out of one convoy. Heineman's overmatched escorts had lost twenty-seven merchantmen in less than three weeks, a crushing blow to the dedicated crews who manned his warships.

But this was just the beginning. Three days after the SC-121 bloodletting, B-Dienst's cryptologists discovered the position and course of convoys SC-122 and HX-229. With Bletchley Park blinded, the best the Allies could do was pinpoint submarines with HuffDuff and guess what their deployment would be. As it became clear the Germans were massing against these two convoys, the Admiralty tried to route them around probable concentrations. The German code breakers uncovered this, which gave Doenitz the chance to shift his patrol lines. His first patrol line missed the lead convoy, SC-122, but no matter. A shift of deployments brought over forty boats into the area. The stage was set for the largest convoy battle of the war.

The Allies faced daunting odds. Convoy SC-122 was protected by the nine escorts of group B-3, which included a frigate, an old flush deck destroyer, a Royal Navy Havant-class destroyer, a cutter, and five *Flower*-class corvettes. Escort Group B-4's five vessels covered down on HX-229's thirty-seven merchantmen.

Above: Two workhorses of the Atlantic War: A USN Consolidated PBY Catalina flying boat and an ASW blimp. Blimps were used by the United States as antisubmarine warfare platforms well into the early 1960s with postwar operations devoted to tracking Soviet submarines. *Left:* A German submarine crew in action.

Above left: Two U-boat skippers smile for the camera. Morale among the skippers and men cracked only once during the war, but it came at a vital moment in the Atlantic. *Above right:* A U-boat crew stalks its prey from periscope depth.

Once again, the Allied escort force faced long odds. At first, weather played against the Germans, and both SC-122 and HX-229 slipped past one of the German patrol lines. Then fickle fate switched sides. Submarine *U-653* left the patrol line early after losing a crewman overboard and having only one nonfunctional torpedo left aboard. While returning to France, the sub stumbled across HX-229 right on the western edge of the Mid-Atlantic Air Gap in the predawn hours of March 16. There was no worse place to be detected, as it gave the Germans the entire gap to maneuver and attack the convoy.

That day, nine U-boats homed in on the convoy, some of which were armed with the new G7e FAT pattern running torpedo. These deadly new weapons were designed to run straight for a preset distance. If it failed to hit a target, it would execute a series of preprogrammed zig-zags until it ran out of endurance or slammed into a target. Against fast-moving warships, this offered no advantage. But if you used one from abeam of a convoy, the torpedo would

zig-zag through columns of slow merchantmen, thus significantly increasing the chance of a hit.

When darkness fell, the nine boats executed their ambush. Seven—*U-603*, *U-384*, *U-435*, *U-600*, *U-758*, *U-91*, and *U-631*—scored that night and following morning. In one attack, *U-600* fired four of the new FAT torpedoes, scoring four hits on three ships, all of which sank.

The attacks continued even after dawn, as the German skippers did not have to fear air attack. Several stragglers were picked off that after breakfast on March 18. Through the rest of the eighteenth and nineteenth, four more merchantmen were destroyed. Before very long-range Liberators arrived to drive the Germans off, HX-229 had lost a third of its ships totaling more than ninety-three thousand tons.

At the same time as HX-229 endured its crucible, the packs set up on SC-122 with singular fury. Discovered by *U-338* on the morning of March 16 about 120 miles east of HX-229, Doenitz sent elements of two patrol groups after this slow convoy. That night, *U-338* waded into the convoy and crept past the escort screen to sink three ships and damage a fourth. Rudolf Bahr's *U-305* picked off two more.

Iceland-based Liberators helped drive off the U-boats, sinking one on the nineteenth. When the battle finally ended on the twentieth, the German boats had destroyed more than 156,000 tons and twenty-one ships in these two convoys. Weather worsened for the final eleven days of the month, which caused attacks and interceptions to taper off. Nevertheless, the total on the month was staggering: 108 ships sunk (most in the north Atlantic) for 585,404 tons. Another 155,615 tons (23 ships) suffered serious damage.

For all the conversations at the Washington Convoy Conference about structure and chains of command and areas of responsibility, the real issue the Allies needed to face had been laid at their feet by Doenitz's boats. The lack of escorts and number of convoys made it a virtual guarantee that the wolf packs would always have the weight of numbers when concentrating on a convoy. Until more escorts could be finished, this dreadful imbalance would continue, and the convoy system itself would be imperiled. In fact, some of the merchant skippers saw the writing on the wall. One freighter commander in HX-229 watched ships explode and sink all around him and decided he'd face better odds alone than in the middle of that onslaught. He ordered full steam and romped away from the convoy, successfully reaching England a few days later.

That sort of indiscipline could spread and grow ever more pervasive, further undermining the convoy system. First and foremost, the merchant marine had to have confidence in it or it simply wouldn't work. And in March 1943, that confidence was tested to the utmost.

HMCS *Barrie*, a Canadian *Flower*-class corvette, seen at sea in 1943. The Canadians played an increasingly important role in the Atlantic starting in late 1942. In 1943, they were given their own independent zone of operation.

CHAPTER THIRTEEN

THE GAME CHANGERS

The boats out fighting these pivotal convoy battles of the beginning of March began to return to France at the end of the month. This meant transiting the Bay of Biscay, where the Allies had laid on Operation Enclose. From March 20 to 28, UK-based long-range aircraft, led by Vickers Wellington bombers equipped with powerful Leigh search lights and brand-new 10cm radar sets, blitzed the U-boat lanes in the bay during the hours of darkness. During those eight days, they spotted twenty-six of the forty-one boats that passed through those waters. They managed to attack fifteen of them and sink one. Not a great record, but the constant threat of air attack, especially at night, strained the U-boat crews even further. By this point in the war, these young German sailors were rarely out of danger. In port, they faced heavy bombing raids that pounded St. Nazaire, Lorient, and Kiel almost every week. Day and night those attacks brought death and destruction to these U-boat enclaves. Once the U-boats were sent to sea, the dangers became manifold. Regardless of the time of day, aircraft could swoop down on them at any moment from the docks at Lorient to the Mid-Atlantic Air Gap thousands of miles away. There was no safe haven from the Allied planes, and the men on watch had to be perfect, lest a mistake like losing concentration or

falling asleep get everyone aboard killed. The pressure was ever-present.

Once in the convoy lanes, the crews faced the escort threat. At times, the sub chasers teamed up with aircraft to tag team the subs, and for that powerful combination the boats had no answer. From January to the end of March, the Allies had managed to sink twenty-five U-boats. That represented more than a quarter of their average monthly strength in the Atlantic. As effective as the U-boats were against the convoys, the fact was the Allies were hammering back—and scoring blows. The deaths of friends, the incessant fear, the stress and tension of every patrol—these were elements toxic to morale. The crews had always carried themselves into battle with great spirit and courage, but their lot was getting harder and their breaks between operations were not enough to let them fully recover before they had to go out again.

At the end of March, convoy HX-230 was picked up by Rudolf Bahr's *U-305*. Bahr had impressed Admiral Doenitz with his tenacity, and *U-305*'s pursuit of HX-230 reinforced his impression of this young officer who was on his first patrol as a skipper.

Based on Bahr's contact report, Doenitz sent more than twenty boats after HX-230. The results were

Opposite: The Vickers Wellington was a veteran of Coastal Command's ASW operations in the Bay of Biscay. Some were later equipped with Leigh search lights and 10cm radar for hunting U-boats at night.

A Coastal Command Beaufighter firing a rocket salvo. *Right:* By the spring of 1943, the Allies began to deploy new antiship and antisubmarine weapons, including the 5-inch rocket. These British-designed projectiles gave a Coastal Command Bristol Beaufighter all the firepower of a fleet destroyer's broadside.

disappointing for the Germans. Submarine *U-610* sank a 7,100-ton American freighter, but that was the only vessel the Allies lost.

In early April, convoy SC-123 arrived at Liverpool after a transit that saw its fifty ships covered by Commander Macintyre's escort group, as well as the new U.S. Navy escort aircraft carrier, USS *Bogue*. The *Bogue*'s arrival in the Atlantic signaled a sea change that would become obvious later in the summer.

Early April saw a lull in the fighting as Doenitz's boats started returning to port to restock their torpedo rooms and load up on fuel and supplies. The maximum effort of the past two months had left his crews exhausted. In fact, toward the end of March and early April, Bletchley Park began reading Doenitz mail again, and in these signals, they detected a decrease in the morale of the

Beaufighters wreaking havoc on a German convoy caught off the coast of Norway. Coastal Command not only was tasked with antisubmarine operations, but also with interdicting the sea lanes to the Third Reich.

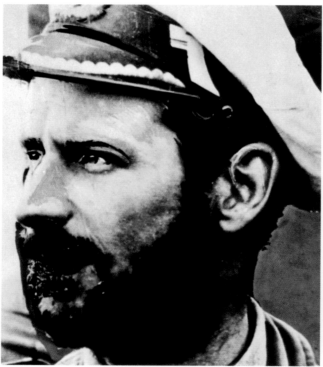

Top: A U-boat under attack by an Allied Liberator. *Above left:* Korevettenkapitän Otto von Bulow looking scruffy and exhausted during a patrol in 1942. He commanded *U-404* during the climactic battles of the Atlantic the following year. On April 23, 1943, he and his crew launched a submerged attack on what they thought was the carrier USS *Ranger*. After hearing four explosions, he reported the American flat-top was probably destroyed. Hitler personally awarded him the Knight's Cross with Oak Leaves for this attack. In fact, *U-404* attacked the escort carrier HMS *Biter*, which suffered no harm. *Above right:* Commander Donald Macintyre ranked as one of Britain's most capable sub killers. He destroyed *U-99* and *U-100* in early 1941, and sank *U-357* in December 1942. He finished the war with six boats to his credit.

Spring 1943 saw the Germans and Allies locked in a titanic series of convoy battles. At times, no fewer than fifty boats descended on inbound convoys, bent on overwhelming the escort screen through sheer numbers. The history of naval warfare has never seen anything like that climax in the Battle of the Atlantic.

submarine crews. There were certain cases where Doenitz apparently suspected his boats did not press their attacks as vigorously as they should have, and the messages sent to his skippers at sea hinted at that.

On April 4, 1943, *U-530* discovered the sixty-one ships of convoy HX-231. Doenitz directed eleven boats to intercept, ordering them to deliver a heavy blow to the Allies. This was unusual. In the past, he could take it on faith that his men would press their attacks to the utmost.

As the month wore on, the cracks in German morale became fissures. Doenitz's messages grew increasingly harsh, and it was obvious to the Bletchley Park folks that something significant was going on within the U-boat fleet. One decoded message had Doenitz telling his men to display "healthy warrior and hunter instincts."

Altogether, the U-boats still at sea sank forty-nine ships totaling about 266,000 tons in April. This was half the total from March, an indicator that the Germans could press the field hard for a while, but could not sustain it indefinitely.

The British smelled an opportunity. Since 1939, the main characteristic of the Atlantic War was the Allies' desperate efforts to avoid encounters with U-boats. Keeping clear of them was the best defense. The Admiralty was tired of running. It was time to bring the U-boats into battle.

That April, the weather improved significantly. The calmer seas meant ASDIC had a better operating environment and could detect submerged submarines more easily. New escort carriers, their air groups full of FM-2 Wildcat fighters and Grumman/General Motors Avenger bombers, had joined the Atlantic fleet. Along with an influx of very-long range bombers, they would soon be able to close the Mid-Atlantic Air Gap once and for all.

At the same time, new technologies began to reach the Allied front-line units in significant numbers. Most important was the new 10cm radar. This was a far more effective system than its predecessors', especially the airborne version. Moreover, the German radar detectors the U-boats used to warn them of approaching Allied

The Germans built 284 U-boats in 1943, but the losses the operational flotillas suffered in the Atlantic in the spring of 1943 were simply crippling. Black May saw Doenitz lose forty-three boats alone. Altogether, the Germans lost 243 boats during what became the decisive year in the Atlantic. More than ten thousand submariners died.

aircraft or escorts could not pick up these new sets. At a crucial juncture, their best early warning system had been rendered useless as an increasing number of escorts and aircraft were fitted with the 10cm radars.

Throughout the war, effective antisubmarine weapons had been an issue for the Allies. The early depth charges had a small blast radius, requiring more accurate drops. Plus, they could not be set to some of the depths that U-boats could actually dive to, a fact the German skippers used to their advantage all the time. By April 1943, however, these deficiencies had been corrected with a new depth charge that had 50 percent more blast power, sank faster, and could be detonated at deeper settings.

Still, the depth charge was a World War I weapon in a new and far more complex environment. What the

Allies needed were new antisubmarine warfare (ASW) weapons to increase their escort's killing power.

The Hedgehog proved to be that weapon.

The biggest drawback to the depth charge was the way it had to be delivered. ASDIC only worked in a forward cone, so when an escort ran down a submerged contact, as it slipped beneath the warship, the ASDIC operators would lose the sub. The escort's skipper had to make his best guess as to when to drop his depth-charge pattern, since his boat would be blind. Afterward, the depth charges exploding created so much turbulence in the water that they neutralized the ASDIC systems for crucial moments. Again, the cagey U-boat skippers often took advantage of this.

The Hedgehog changed the game entirely. Mounted on the bow of an escort, this new weapon was a box

Left: Commander Frederic "Johnnie" Walker prosecuting a U-boat contact aboard his escort, HMS *Starling*. He and his escort group sank more boats than any other Allied commander, but he gave his last full measure to the cause. His son was killed in 1943 while serving aboard a submarine in the Mediterranean, and he literally worked himself to death in the Atlantic the following year. After sinking six U-boats in ten days in June 1944, he suffered cerebral thrombosis while at sea and died two days later at age forty-eight. *Below:* HMS *Miralda* in the Atlantic with a Swordfish spotted on deck. The *Miralda* started life as a Dutch tanker, but it was rebuilt as a merchant aircraft carrier—a British stop-gap design. These vessels fell somewhere between the CAM ships and escort carriers. Capable of carrying four Swordfish for antisubmarine warfare work, they could carry out air operations while simultaneously carrying cargo to Britain. Crewed by civilian merchant seamen, they had Royal Navy and Fleet Air Arm contingents aboard to man the weapons systems and handle flight operations. Nineteen in three different classes were built during the war.

Above: A pair of Grumman Avengers in flight. The Avenger was the largest carrier-based aircraft built by the United States during the war, but its docile handling characteristics made it ideally suited for operating off the narrow, shorter decks that characterized the U.S. Navy's escort carriers.

Opposite: A pair of FM-2 Wildcats during landing operations aboard an escort carrier in the Atlantic. In U.S. Navy doctrine, when escort carriers went hunting for U-boats, they would send a mixed force of Avengers and Wildcats aloft. The FM-2s were supposed to sweep in first to machine gun the U-boat and suppress its antiaircraft defenses. Then the Avengers would roll in to finish the sub off with depth charges, homing torpedoes, and rockets or bombs.

containing twenty-four projectiles, each weighing thirty-two pounds. When a submarine was detected under the surface, the escort would steam straight for it, then trigger all twenty-four projectiles at once. They would arc out in front of the escort and drop into the ocean in a circular, thirty meter–wide pattern. They were contact-fused, meaning they would not explode unless they hit the targeted U-boat, thus sparing the escort of the ASDIC blackout caused by depth charges.

Production of the Hedgehog began in late 1941, but it took almost a year to see widespread deployment aboard Allied escort vessels. Early use of the new weapon saw inexperienced crews make lots of mistakes. Only about 5 percent of the Hedgehog attacks scored kills at first. But as crews received better training on them, their effectiveness skyrocketed. The Hedgehog became one of the key U-boat killing technologies of World War II.

The increased number of aircraft patrolling the Atlantic received an influx of new equipment and weaponry that early spring as well. Airborne 10cm radar sets became more common, allowing the Leigh light Wellingtons and other aircraft to find, fix, and sink U-boats with incredible accuracy in bad weather and at night. More Liberator bombers, modified with additional fuel tanks to extend their range, were able to reach into all but the very deepest parts of the

THE MOST FAMOUS COASTIE

In 1937, Chief Boatswain Mate A. A. "Blackie" Rother went on shore leave from the U.S. Coast Guard cutter USS *Campbell*. While out on the town, he picked up a mix-breed black-and-tan pup with an odd splash of white on its chest. He took the dog over to his girlfriend's place to give him to her as present. Not such a good idea: her building did not allow pets.

Unwilling to dump the pup, Rother took him bar hopping, and the canine quickly impressed Blackie's shipmates. He drank coffee, slammed shots of whiskey with the boys, and quaffed beer with the best of them. The coasties were so taken by him that they officially enlisted the dog into the coast guard. Named Sinbad, the pup left his paw print on his enlistment papers and received his own Red Cross identification number. He was brought aboard ship, given his own bunk, had his own duty stations, and served with distinction as the *Campbell*'s chief dog.

Sinbad was promoted several times, busted in rank as a result of infractions, and officially disciplined twice. Once World War II broke out, Sindbad was assigned to damage control below decks as his battle station. He stayed with the *Campbell*'s crew throughout the war and became the most celebrated coast guard veteran of the Atlantic campaign. Featured in magazines and newspapers throughout the United States, Sinbad's story won over dog lovers from coast to coast. The USS *Campbell* was inundated with well-wishing letters for Sinbad, some of which included photos of letter writers' own pets.

While loved at home, Sinbad caused several international incidents with America's allies in Greenland and North Africa during stays in port. One *Life* magazine article described him as a "liberty-rum-chow-hound, with a bit of bulldog, doberman pinscher, and what-not. Mostly what-not."

During port calls, Sinbad was first off the *Campbell*, and he'd lead the crew down to the local dive bars, where he had long since learned to jump atop the stools and await his shot of whiskey. Once he finished his booze, he'd hop off and head to the next bar, the rest of the crew in tow.

Sinbad was a salty sailor to the core. Though he had his own bunk, he would sleep snug against a different coastie almost every night. He avoided officers like the plague and almost never socialized with them, except for a few rare occasions while drinking ashore.

He missed movement once in Sicily, an infraction for which he was busted in rank, and had to be delivered to the *Campbell* by the shore patrol.

During the violent convoy battles in February 1943, the USS *Campbell* was part of an escort group that was overwhelmed by a U-boat wolf pack. As ship after ship went down, the *Campbell*'s crew fought it out for days with the German subs. On the night of February 22, 1943, the *Campbell* dueled it out with a Type VII boat, *U-606*. After depth charging the German sub to the surface with the help of a Polish destroyer, the *Campbell*'s skipper turned and rammed the U-boat, sending her to the bottom.

Mid-Atlantic Air Gap. Instead of carrying bombs or depth charges, in May 1943, these aircraft began carrying the Mark 24 Mine, a deliberately deceptive name for what was actually the first antisubmarine passive array acoustic torpedo. Designed and developed by the Harvard Underwater Sound Lab and Bell Telephone, the Mark 24 homed in on a submarine's turning screws.

This revolutionary new weapon became the first in a long series of such weapons that are still in use today.

At the end of April, convoy ONS-5 sailed from Liverpool with forty-three ships under the escort of Group B-7. The convoy was routed northward to maximize the amount of air cover it could receive from Iceland while en route to Halifax, Canada.

The *Campbell* survived the collision but lost power and began taking on water. Captain James Hirschfield ordered all but a skeleton crew to abandon ship. Most of the men took to the boats and were transferred to other vessels. A few stayed with the skipper to try to keep the ship afloat as it was towed to Canada. Among the crew who remained aboard was Sinbad. He sustained the men's morale as they sustained their ship. *Campbell* survived the collision, was repaired, and was sent back into action. Later in 1944, Sinbad still aboard, the cutter was strafed and bombed by Luftwaffe aircraft while in the Mediterranean.

Sinbad survived the war and was the first U.S. Coast Guard sailor to ever have a biography written about him. He went on a book tour and retired from the service with eleven years of service and a final rank of chief dog (K9C). He died in 1951 at his retirement home, the Barnegat Lighthouse on the Jersey shore, where he was known to still frequent the local bars and drink with the boys.

The USS *Campbell* survived until 1984 after serving in three wars with considerable distinction. She was sunk as a target in the Pacific after her crew fired off one last radio transmission, which read in part:

> *I served with honor for almost forty-six years, in war and peace, in the Atlantic and Pacific. With duty as diverse as saving lives to sinking U-boats, ocean stations to fisheries enforcement, and from training cadets to being your flagship. I have been always ready to serve.*

The PBM Mariner served as the stablemate to the PBY Catalina in the U.S. Navy's arsenal of ship-killing flying boats. Mariners equipped almost thirty navy squadrons during the war, as well as coast guard and foreign units. They sank ten U-boats during the Atlantic war.

On April 28, 1943, *U-650* detected and reported the convoy's position. Doenitz wanted to score a decisive victory this time, and he had the boats to do it. Some fifty were in the waters around ONS-5. B-Dienst tracked the convoy, while at the same time Bletchley Park's intelligence dried up again after the Germans changed their codes on the twenty-fifth. The Germans started this battle with all the pieces in place to inflict unprecedented carnage.

What could fifty boats do?

From April 29, 1943, until May 6, the German subs piled on the convoy as Doenitz barraged them with messages demanding his skippers press the Allies at all costs.

His men did their best. On the first night of the engagement, three boats tried to get past the escort screen. Equipped with the 10cm radar sets, the ships of B-7 easily picked up all three U-boats as they tried to sneak up to the convoy on the surface. The British

Every landing craft that took part in Allied amphibious invasions in the European Theater had to cross the Atlantic. Some sailed independently. Others were carried across, lashed to decks of larger cargo ships.

warships counterattacked and damaged all three U-boats before they could do any serious harm to the convoy.

The tactics of 1940 simply failed before the technology of 1943.

When the night surface attacks didn't work, *U-258* switched things up, submerged at dawn and struck the convoy at 0930 the next morning. One freighter went down.

The Germans had drawn blood now, but later that afternoon a patrolling PBY Catalina from VP-84 damaged *U-528*.

The Admiralty was under no illusions at what was about to happen here. The HuffDuff-equipped ships and aircraft around the convoy picked up a shocking number

of contacts all converging on ONS-5, and it looked like the escort would be swamped and overwhelmed, just like what had happened to Heineman's group earlier in the year.

There was a short respite as the Germans lost contact with the convoy as bad weather struck the area. Some of the boats that had joined the pursuit broke off to go try to intercept SC-128, but they had little luck with that. They were sent to intercept ONS-5 again.

On May 4, an RCAF patrol plane discovered and sank *U-630* some thirty miles behind the convoy. Three other U-boats also underwent air attack. Meanwhile, the storm-tossed seas scattered the convoy. Stragglers abounded, and B-7's warships had to race around

Above: An FM-2 Wildcat aboard the escort carrier USS *Core*. During her first two hunter-killer patrols in 1943, the *Core*'s air group sank five U-boats while one of her escorts sank a sixth. Such was the devastating ASW power of these small carriers. *Below:* Operating off escort carriers required considerable skill and focus, especially in bad weather. But even in the best conditions, accidents were common. Here, a Grumman Avenger goes over the side of an escort aircraft carrier in one such accident. Note the pilot is trying to get his turret gunner out of their sinking aircraft. The photo was taken in early 1943.

Right: One of the USS *Core*'s Wildcat pilots poses before his FM-2 in November 1943 during the carrier's second hunter-killer patrol in the Atlantic. *Below:* On August 7, 1943, an Avenger pilot from the USS *Card* attacked *U-66* while she refueled from a milch cow (*U-117*). He scored this near miss on *U-66* (at left), which survived the blast. The milch cow was not so lucky. Subsequent attacks crippled her, and several other arriving Avengers finished her off. It took three homing torpedoes and eight depth charges to get the job done. Another task force sank *U-66* only a few months after her narrow escape here.

An Avenger from *Core* conducts a daylight ASW patrol in July 1943 during the carrier's first hunter-killer operation. The ship's aircraft sank *U-487* and *U-67* that month, a spectacularly successful initiation to the war in the Atlantic.

looking for them. The U-boats picked off six stranglers before help could arrive.

The attacks continued even as the weather worsened. The next day, submerged daylight attacks sank four more merchantmen. The Allied airmen assigned to protect the convoy went to heroic lengths to do so. One Newfoundland-based Canadian Catalina crashed as a result of the heavy fog and rain, killing its crew. Another Catalina managed to get aloft. They searched for the convoy for hours, but could not locate it in the murk. Meanwhile, as ships were going down, a VLR Liberator from Iceland flew over a thousand miles from its base and found ONS-5. It stayed overhead as long

as it could, but the weather once again hampered the aviators. Flying through the storm, the crew could see little of what was happening below them. All too soon, their fuel ran low and they were forced to turn for home.

When darkness fell that evening, fifteen U-boats were stalking the convoy. Throughout the night, they made twenty-six attempts to penetrate the screen and get in amongst the merchant ships. The outnumbered escorts went into a frenzy, racing back and forth along the convoy's flanks and rear as they chased down boats their 10cm radars detected. HMS *Sunflower* thwarted four attacks with quick counter charges that drove off the U-boats and damaged one of them. At the same time,

HMS *Premier*, a *Bogue*-class escort aircraft carrier was built in Seattle then transferred to the Royal Navy in 1943. She is seen here in 1944 on a ferry run to England carrying a full deck of Lend-Lease Chance-Vought F4U Corsairs and Grumman Avengers.

the HMS *Loosestrife* depth charged and sank *U-192*.

At one point during the night of the May 5 and early morning of May 6, the *Flower*-class corvette HMS *Snowflake* spotted three U-boats making a coordinated drive at the convoy proper. The plucky crew chased all three down and blew *U-531* to the surface with depth charges. Later, HMS *Vidette* finished that sub off with a Hedgehog salvo.

When *U-125* tried to get into an attack position, the destroyer HMS *Oribi* rammed the sub. The *Snowflake* joined in the attack and sank the sub with her deck guns. The entire German crew went down with their boat when the British escorts received orders not to pick up enemy survivors. There would be no mercy on this night.

The crew of the *Snowflake* wasn't finished. After spotting *U-535* on the surface, the skipper rammed her too. She was later sunk by depth charges from the HMS *Vidette*.

On the morning of May 6, ONS-5 received further reinforcements for its escort screen. Already, the 3rd Support Group's escorts, the HMS *Oribi* being one of them, had arrived to plus up the screen. Now, the 3rd Support Group reached the battle, adding two sloops and three frigates to the fray.

They went straight into action as ONS-5 steamed into waters peppered with icebergs. One escort, sloop HMS *Pelican*, made radar contact with two bergs and her crew thought they were surfaced U-boats. They sped toward the contacts, only to discover the towering icebergs at

The sensor system that changed the entire dynamic of the Atlantic Campaign. The 10cm surface search radar set gave Allied aircraft a tremendous advantage over the U-boats in 1943. Able to pinpoint subs even when not fully surfaced, they were far more accurate and useful than previous airborne radar systems. Just as important, the sets could not be picked up by the German Metox radar warning receivers carried by U-boats in 1943. This allowed Allied planes to stalk surfaced subs at night undetected, then swoop down to attack their unsuspecting targets.

Above: U-66 and U-117 on the surface under attack by USS Core's aircraft. Thanks to Anglo-American code-breaking efforts, the Allies pinpointed where the rendezvous points were for Doenitz's milch cows. Knowing that these resupply subs played a key role in extending the endurance of other U-boats, the Allies hunted these subs down ruthlessly through the second half of 1943. By the end of the year, eleven of the fourteen milch cows in the Atlantic had been sunk. Right: An Avenger after a hard landing aboard Ranger in March 1943.

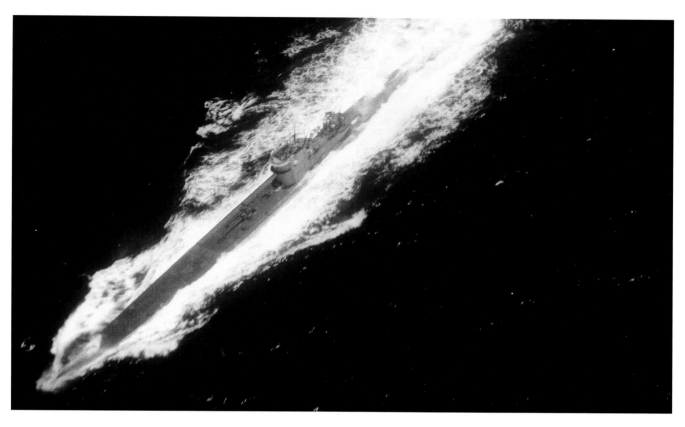

U-185, a Type IXC long-range boat, under attack on August 24, 1943, by USS *Core's* air group. She went down with twenty-nine of her crew (twenty-two survived). This actually was the fourth air attack *U-185* had endured since starting its third patrol in June—an indicator of just how dangerous it was to operate in the Atlantic in mid-1943.

the last minute and narrowly avoided a *Titanic* moment both times.

A third radar contact proved to be *U-438*, which the *Pelican* depth charged and sank. There were no survivors.

Another sloop from the 3rd Support Group drove off *U-575* with its deck guns. Damaged, the boat broke contact and limped away.

That morning, Doenitz gave the order to break off the onslaught. In one night of furious fighting, he had lost seven of his gray wolves to Allied escorts. The total came to nine when two more, *U-439* and *U-659*, collided in the fog and sank.

In return, the subs destroyed thirteen merchantmen during the entire effort against ONS-5. The Germans

had done given their full measure for Doenitz and had barely scored more than a one-to-one loss rate for the effort. It was a decisive defeat, one that signaled the turning of the tide. The rest of May reinforced that.

It wasn't numbers that made the difference in the end; it was the new technology that stemmed the U-boat slaughters. The 10cm radar made even the most ancient escorts a powerful threat now. They could pinpoint even as small an object as a periscope from miles away with these new sets, and the Germans had no counter for it. Unjammed and undetected, the 10cm radar gave the Allies unerring eyes in the darkness and ensured they would have opportunities to use their new weapons.

Between May 10 and 24, 370 ships passed through the Atlantic Air Gap, the prime hunting ground of Doenitz's

As crucial as escorts were to the survival of the merchant ships, they were essentially defensive warships, tasked with guarding the convoys as they crossed the Atlantic. Carrier-based aircraft gave the allies the offensive dimension they needed to take the war directly to Doenitz's wolves.

wolves. Six were sunk. In return, FIDO-armed aircraft, along with escorts carrying the new depth charges and Hedgehogs, sank thirteen boats.

The Allies went on the attack. The Bay of Biscay became a nightmare to cross, forcing the U-boats to stay submerged as much as possible. Aircraft roamed the skies day and night. Escort carrier groups swept the flanks of convoys. The USS *Bogue*'s Avengers and Wildcats scored their first kill when they caught and sank *U-569* on May 22, 1943.

By the end of the month, the Germans had lost forty-one boats. In less than thirty days, the Allies had turned the North Atlantic into a mass graveyard for Doenitz's

men. From this point on, the hunters would be the hunted.

Doenitz's force was crushed by this disaster, and on May 24, 1943, he ordered his boats out of the North Atlantic. In the past, these strategic redeployments had found weak areas upon which to prey, and he hoped to do this again in the mid-Atlantic against the Africa-bound convoys.

Not this time. Allied aircraft and warships sank 18 more submarines in June and another 38 in July. Another 24 went down in August. In four months, the Kriegsmarine lost 121 U-boats. There would be no recovery from these blows. The Germans had lost the Battle of the Atlantic.

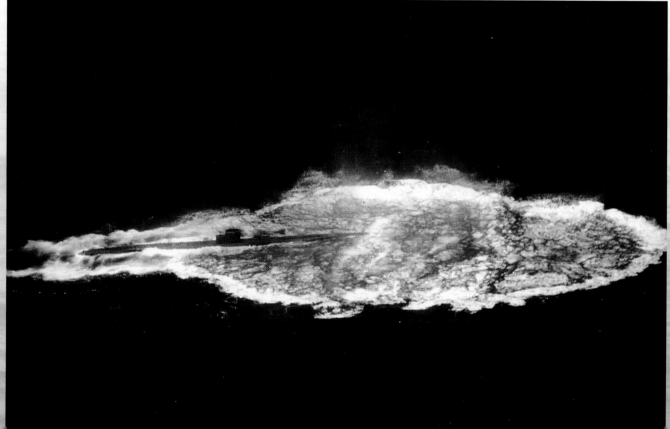

The U.S. Navy capture of *U-505* on June 4, 1944, was a closely guarded secret so that Germany would not know an Enigma machine and code books were in the hands of the Allies. *Chris Sheppard*

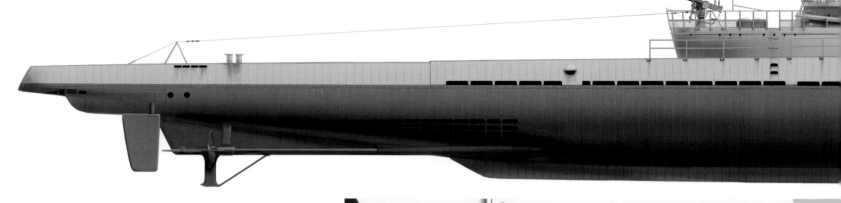

Right: After Black May, Doenitz realized his boats stood no chance in the Atlantic. Allied aircraft, technology, and escorts had overcome all the advantages his crews once enjoyed. He had hoped to counter these developments with new technologies of his own, but they were slow to arrive. The snorkel was one such innovation. It allowed a sub to run on its diesel engines and recharge its batteries while submerged. It reached operational service by early 1944.
Below: When Italy surrendered in September 1943, dozens of submarines and surface ships were removed from the strategic equation in the Mediterranean and Atlantic. Here, American sailors board one of the Italian navy's submarines after it surrendered at Salerno.

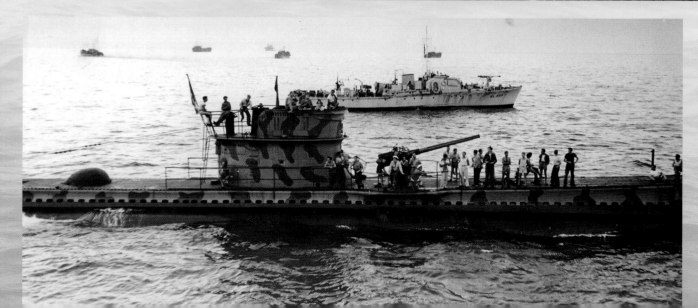

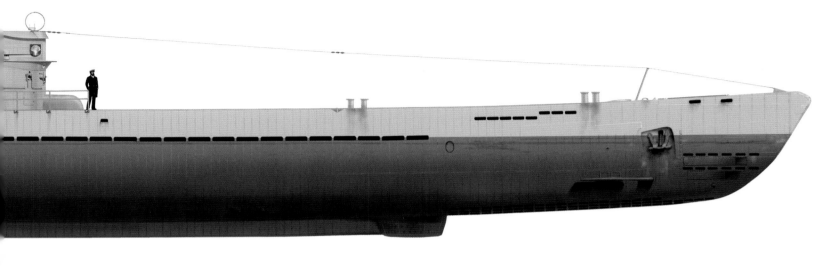

Above: Ace Erich Topp's final wartime command, the Type XXI boat *U-2513*. Doenitz had hoped the new Type XXIs could turn the tide in the Atlantic as the new subs could stay beneath the waves for up to three days at a time. They could recharge their batteries from the boat's snorkel in only five hours, minimizing their exposure to Allied surface search radar while doing so. They were so quiet that captured Type XXIs became the basis for the first Cold War–era American and British submarines. *Left:* A Type XXI under attack by British aircraft in the final days of the war. Only 2 of the 118 built carried out war patrols before V-E Day.

EPILOGUE

The convoys got through; the tonnage war was over. England became the great base from which the Allies launched the Normandy invasion. The vast fleet that delivered the armies to France was virtually immune to naval attack as it crossed the Channel and loitered off Normandy's shores. The victory in the Atlantic in the spring and summer of 1943 set the conditions for the campaign in northwest Europe.

All Adm. Karl Doenitz could do was to try to delay the inevitable. He continued the U-boat campaign right to the end of the war, hoping new technologies and new submarines, such as the Type XXI, could change the equation at sea as dramatically as the Allies had done with their new systems in the spring of 1943. But it was too late. Despite some creative designs, technology (such as the Schnorkel that allowed boats to recharge their batteries while submerged), new homing torpedoes, and more, the Germans could never find an answer to Allied air power. Once the skies above the U-boats were owned by well-armed Liberators, Sunderlands, Mariners, and Avengers, the boats stood little chance. The loss rate continued, and the number of merchant ships sunk plummeted. In the final months of the war, the U-boats were sinking one freighter for every two subs lost.

By May 1945, Doenitz had lost 759 U-boats. Seventy-five percent of the men under his command were killed or captured—some thirty thousand out of forty thousand who wore the uniform of the U-boat arm. No other branch of service suffered such devastating losses. At times, their morale wavered, but it never broke despite the lessening chances of survival as the war ground on. They went out to sea time after time, knowing that every cargo ship they sank meant one less delivery of weapons, ammunition, bombs, planes, and tanks that could be used against their homeland. The men of the U-boat arm remained faithful to their cause to the final day of the war.

To keep the sea lanes to Britain open cost the Allies seventy-five thousand men. Through the course of the war, the Germans had sunk more than two thousand merchantmen and almost two hundred warships. Without the courage and steadfast dedication of the civilian merchant seamen, the Allied cause would have been lost. The final victory against Nazism and all its attendant horrors came on their anonymous backs. It started and ended in the Atlantic. Without their willingness to sail into treacherous waters, Britain and Russia would not have been sustained in their darkest hours. The invasions

The final surrender. Only a fraction of the U-boat crews who served in the Atlantic survived the war. The men aboard this sub were some of the lucky few.

Above: In the postwar years, historians and writers who have chronicled the Battle of the Atlantic have focused much of their effort on the U-boat aces. The small number of aces sank the majority of the Allied shipping lost during the war, a testament to their skill, daring, and professionalism. Yet, emphasis on their exploits has come at a cost. Few books have been written about the heroes of the merchant marine, and seventy years later most of their remarkable acts of courage—bravery that sustained the Allied cause—have been lost to history.
Right: William Arthur Oxford, age twenty: one of the thousands of anonymous, civilian heroes whose shoulders carried the Allied armies to the heart of the Third Reich and ultimate victory.

of North Africa, Sicily, Italy, and France could not have happened. There would have been no fuel-gobbling dash by Patton's Third Army to the German frontier in the fall of 1944. There would have been no avgas, no bombs, or no ammunition for the aerial campaign against the Third Reich's cities and industries.

When the war came to a blessed end, this achievement was all but crushed from popular memory under the weight of so many other "glorious" aspects of the war—fighter aces, daring air battles, Monty and Bradley, the Bulge, Stalingrad, Omaha Beach. These moments defined the perception generations to come would have of World War II. There was no glamour to be found in the Atlantic's long and grinding campaign. There was no larger-than-life character like MacArthur in the merchant marine to garner headlines and remind people that the war was won on the churning Atlantic. And so, the merchant marine got short-changed. They came home without fanfare, pieced together their lives

as best they could. In quiet moments, they remembered the horrors to which they bore witness and mourned their lost friends and shipmates with quiet reverence. They were all but forgotten by their nations and by those chronicling the campaigns of World War II. There was little money to be made writing about cargo ships going down, so the writers and historians flocked to the other, more lucrative aspects of the war. No Stephen Ambrose stepped forward to resurrect their contribution or celebrate their role in the victory. Perhaps some of them waited, hoping for that to change at some point. But it never did. There would be no merchant marine *Band of Brothers* or a nautical *Saving Private Ryan* to awake the public.

Ultimately, these remarkable men died as they had fought—anonymously, part of an aggregate that had helped redefine the world and then went home to a life of quiet toil in suburbs and cities.

History can be unbearably cruel.

BIOGRAPHICAL NOTES

Hundreds of talented historians and writers have spilled considerable ink writing about the North Atlantic campaign. Among the best survey accounts are Peter Padfield's *War Beneath the Sea: Submarine Conflict During World War II*. John Terraine's *The U-Boat Wars: 1916–1945* provides perspective and comparisons with the first undersea campaign during World War I. Correlli Barnett's work on the Royal Navy during World War II, *Engage the Enemy More Closely*, is an absolute masterpiece and a must read for anyone interested in how the British navy endured the crucible of World War II. Marc Milner's *Battle of the Atlantic* is another outstanding survey of the campaign, as is *Bitter Ocean: The Battle of the Atlantic, 1939–1945* by David Fairbank White. Of course, anyone interested in World War II naval warfare must read Samuel Eliot Morison's *History of United States Naval Operations in World War II*. Volume I and Volume X cover the American side of the Atlantic War.

For specific periods and battles within the Atlantic campaign there are many fine works. Michael Gannon's *Black May: The Epic Story of the Allies' Defeat of the German U-Boats in May 1943*, Ed Offley's *Turning the Tide*, and Gannon's *Operation Drumbeat* are fantastic, spirited accounts of key episodes in the Atlantic.

There are so many outstanding first-person accounts of the fighting that one could spend years reading them. Noteworthy are Donald Macintyre's memoir, *The Battle of the Atlantic*, and Hans Goebeler's *Steel Boats, Iron Hearts: The Wartime Saga of Hans Goebeler and the U-505*. Robert Carse's *There Go the Ships* provides a vivid look into the lives of merchant sailors and the fighting in the Arctic.

The code war has attracted many devoted researchers and historians. You can't go wrong with Jim DeBrosse and Colin Burke's *The Secret in Building 26: The Untold Story of America's Ultra War Against the U-Boat Enigma Codes*. F. W. Winterbotham's classic *The Ultra Secret* remains a must read in the field. F. H. Hinsley and Alan Stripp's *Codebreakers: The Inside Story of Bletchley Park* provides rich insight into the daily struggles the men and women there faced.

INDEX

Mark One eyeball, 30, 83
Metox radar warning receivers, 287
Oerlikon, 17
quadruple AA guns, 261
Schnorkel, 295
Type 286M radar array, 128

GENERAL INDEX